Praise for *Encountering the Lord in the Gospel of Mark*

"There is no better way to read Mark's Gospel than slowly and reflectively, from beginning to end, over a period of days. And there is no better guide for this journey than Leo Zanchettin, whose work proves that he's been in conversation with this gospel for many years. Even his writing style mimics that of Mark: short pithy sentences, filled with vivid imagery, all connected together in a way that keeps the reader moving along with the vibrant message of this good news. So give yourself a break, and let Leo Zanchettin become your retreat master for a thirty-day transforming experience with Jesus."
—**Stephen J. Binz, writer, speaker, and pilgrimage leader at Bridge-B.com**

"This little book packs a much-needed punch for the modern Christian. In simple yet profound reflections, Leo Zanchettin takes the reader on an engaging and fast-paced tour through the Gospel of St. Mark. His insights into various verses and scenes will give a Scriptural novice an incredible starting point and theological veterans a new perspective. I thoroughly enjoyed this book and highly suggest to anyone looking to kickstart their own personal (or group) Bible study time. What a gift to the modern believer."
—**Mark Hart, executive vice president of Life Teen and author of the *Something More Faith Series***

"What better way to ta ing in the word of God? Leo ights,

D1636968

and thought-provoking questions draw readers into the heart of the good news of Christ. A fantastic resource for taking a life-changing deep dive into the Gospel according to St. Mark."
—Mary Healy, professor of Sacred Scripture at Sacred Heart Major Seminary

"People sometimes ask me, 'What's your favorite Gospel?,' and I always say 'Mark.' This wonderful book reminds me why. With clarity and compassion, and the wisdom of a patient teacher, Leo Zanchettin unpacks Mark's Gospel and helps us see it with new eyes and new hearts. What a treasure! *Encountering the Lord in the Gospel of Mark* is a real gift for personal reflection, for prayer groups, and even for preachers who might be looking for ideas to kickstart their homilies. Add this to your library. You can thank me later!"
—Deacon Greg Kandra, blogger and author of *The Busy Person's Guide to Prayer*

"Leo Zanchettin points out that in Mark's telling of the good news, the people Jesus called to be closest to him—his disciples—often failed to have faith in him, understand his teaching, or persevere with him to the end. The real heroes are the men and women who appear only briefly, the 'minor characters' who do put their faith in Jesus and experience the healing and life he wants to give. With fresh commentary and thoughtful questions for reflection, *Encountering the Lord in the Gospel of Mark* can help every reader enter into Mark's Gospel and become one of those 'minor characters' today."
—Kevin Perrotta, author of the *Six Weeks with the Bible* series

Encountering the Lord in the Gospel of Mark

A 30-Day At-Home Retreat

Leo Zanchettin

theWORD
among us®
press

Published by The Word Among Us Press
7115 Guilford Drive, Suite 100
Frederick, Maryland 21704

wau.org

25 24 23 22 21   1 2 3 4 5

ISBN: 978-1-59325-557-2
eISBN: 978-1-59325-559-6

Design by Suzanne Earl

Made and printed in the United States of America

Library of Congress Control Number: 2021916849

Contents

Setting the Stage

Mark 1:1

The beginning . . . (Mark 1:1)

From the very start of his Gospel, St. Mark leaves nothing to chance. In fact, his first line reveals everything you need to know about the story he is going to tell:

> The beginning of the good news of Jesus Christ, the Son of God. (1:1)

There it is. Mark's entire Gospel in one sentence. It comes and goes so quickly that we might skim right over it. *I know this already. Jesus Christ is the Son of God. It's in the Creed we say every Sunday at Mass.* But within this one sentence is a universe of meaning—a universe filled with promise for anyone who delves into it.

Look Again

The beginning. Mark doesn't say anything about Jesus' birth, as Matthew and Luke do. There's no annunciation, no journey to Bethlehem, no manger, no swaddling clothes. Joseph isn't mentioned by name at all.

It's not that these events are unimportant. It's that Mark is telling the story of Jesus from a different angle. For Mark, the good news "begins" when Jesus arrives at the Jordan River for baptism by John.

Jesus Christ, the Son of God. Mark is going to tell us about Jesus. And he will do so by telling his story in two acts. Act One (chapters 1–8) will focus on Jesus as Christ, and Act Two (chapters 9–16) will focus on Jesus as Son of God. In both acts, he will tell us what kind of person Jesus is: what kind of Christ he is, first, and then how Jesus lived—and died—as the Son of God.

But Why?

But why undertake such a project at all? What prompted Mark to write? There's one obvious answer and one not-so-obvious answer.

First, the more obvious answer: something had to be done. It had been around thirty years since Jesus' death and resurrection when Mark wrote his Gospel. Jesus had returned to heaven and commanded his disciples to "go into all the world and proclaim the good news to the whole creation" (Mark 16:15). And that's precisely what they did. Through the preaching of Peter, John, James, and the others—and a little later, through Paul, Barnabas, and even Mark himself—people all over the known world had come to believe in Jesus.

But now, thirty years later, the apostles were beginning to die off. James was the first, executed by Herod as early as A.D. 44 (Acts 12:2). Then, most dramatically, Peter and Paul were martyred in Rome between A.D. 65 and 69. Other apostles had set out for distant lands where they too met a martyr's death: Thomas in India, Andrew in Greece, and Simon and Jude in Syria.

With so many firsthand witnesses gone, the churches in major cities like Rome and Jerusalem and Antioch were left with second- and third-generation leaders. The line of continuity between themselves and the original apostles remained intact, but memories were fading. Future generations needed something trustworthy to help them grasp who Jesus was and why he was so important. So someone—namely Mark—needed to commit the apostles' teaching to writing.

The not-so-obvious reason? The disappearance of the first apostles created a vacuum. And into that vacuum stepped people of all stripes. They came with their own stories about Jesus—some accurate, others not so much. The stories and testimonies about Jesus began to meld and become confused. Many of them portrayed Jesus as a different kind of Christ and a different kind of Son of God than Jesus truly was. And that difference was causing division and scandal.

So Mark decided to do something about it, and the result is the Gospel we are going to read through and pray about over the next month.

But Who?

But who was Mark? Tradition holds that he was the same John Mark who accompanied Paul and Barnabas on their first missionary journey but who returned home before the mission was complete (Acts 13:5; 15:36-39). Church Fathers also identify him with the cousin of Barnabas, whom Paul mentions in Colossians 4:10, and as the same Mark whom Paul mentions as a co-worker in 2 Timothy 4:11 and Philemon 24. Finally, Peter refers to "my son Mark" at the end of his first letter (5:13).

It's quite plausible that all these verses refer to the same Mark who wrote this Gospel. But at the same time, the name Mark (*Markos* in Greek and *Marcus* in Latin) was even more common in the first century A.D. than it is today. Not to mention, Mark never identifies himself in his Gospel. So this Mark could be any number of other figures. The short answer is that we don't exactly know who he was.

What we do know, however, is that the Mark of this Gospel is a master storyteller. His is the shortest of the four Gospels—he tells far fewer stories than the others. But the stories he does tell are filled with rich, dramatic details that have the power to move us to prayer and deeper self-reflection.

We also know that this Mark tells a story filled with conflict and tension. Early on in his ministry, Jesus' teachings and miracles elicit condemnation and even hatred from many of Israel's religious leaders (see 3:6). Mark portrays Jesus' family as being not just confused about his mission but worried that he is "out of his mind" (3:21). Even Jesus' closest disciples appear more stubborn and slow to believe than they do in the other Gospels (see 4:40). The threat of death casts a long shadow, and as the Gospel progresses, Jesus becomes increasingly misunderstood, rejected, and isolated. In the end, he dies completely alone with just a few women keeping vigil "from a distance" (15:40).

Jesus, and Jesus alone, is the focus of Mark's Gospel. In every chapter, Mark asks us to decide whether we will stay with Jesus or join the other characters in resisting him, rebuking him, or outright rejecting him.

Good News?

Master storyteller. Innovative creator of a new style of writing. Protector of Jesus' legacy. Challenger of the status quo. Mark is an impressive figure. But there is another title he deserves, and that's the title he has borne for nearly two thousand years: *Evangelist*. Proclaimer of the good news of the gospel.

In his opening line, Mark tells us that the story he is about to relate is the *good news* about Jesus (1:1). But we might wonder what's so good about Mark's story. Jesus' closest disciples struggle to believe in him. Religious leaders hate him. His own family tries to "restrain" him, and he dies alone (3:21). Even the women who come to the tomb to anoint his body are so terrified by the angel that they fail to carry out his command to tell the apostles about Jesus' resurrection (see 16:8).

So just what is the good news that Mark wants to tell us? That's the question we want to explore for the next thirty days. As we pray together through the Gospel of Mark, we'll discover more than enough evidence that his story is filled with good news. But it doesn't come from the main characters surrounding Jesus—his disciples or his family. It comes from the minor characters who appear for a scene or two, then disappear into the background. It comes from the outsiders and the ones who, like Jesus, suffered rejection and isolation:

- A woman suffering from hemorrhages in Mark 5 whose faith is so strong that she needs only to touch Jesus' cloak to be healed.
- The father of a boy with epilepsy in Mark 9 who humbly admits his unbelief and cries out for help.
- The men in Mark 2 who believe in Jesus enough to want to tear up a roof and lower their friend down on a stretcher for Jesus to heal him.

- And most of all, there's the centurion at the cross—a pagan soldier who may well have been one of the men who mocked and scourged Jesus—making the clearest and most convincing confession of faith in the whole Gospel: "Truly this man was God's Son!" (15:39).

These are the heroes of Mark's Gospel. It's their stories that we will examine. Because in the end, their stories are our stories. Only as we become like them will we discover the true goodness of the gospel we believe. And only as we become like them will we discover the goodness and love of Jesus, who is the Christ and the Son of God.

In on the Secret

Mark 1:2-13

*The Spirit immediately drove him out into the
wilderness. (Mark 1:12)*

I'm going to ask you to do something today that I'd like
you to do every day during this retreat: *read* the passage.
Read it slowly, prayerfully, carefully. We can be so familiar
with the stories in the Gospels that we dive right into the
commentary looking for the meat of the message. But I promise you, the best I can offer you are a couple of side dishes.
Of course, I hope they'll be good side dishes and that they
will complement the main course well. But just as creamy
mashed potatoes are just a lump of white . . . stuff . . . without a fine cut of rib eye, the commentaries here won't give
you the full experience. You need to read the passage!

An Intimate Message

Okay, now that we've cleared that up, let's take a look at these verses. Did you notice how Mark seems to skim over the stories of Jesus' baptism and his temptation in the desert—especially when compared to Matthew's and Luke's accounts? He doesn't tell us what John the Baptist actually said, as Luke does. And he doesn't relate the details of the devil's temptations, as both Matthew and Luke do. But he does let us in on a secret:

> Just as [Jesus] was coming up out of the water, he saw the heavens torn apart and the Spirit descending like a dove on him. And a voice came from heaven, "You are my Son, the Beloved; with you I am well pleased." (1:10-11)

Notice the wording: *Jesus* saw the heavens torn open; *Jesus* saw the Spirit coming like a dove; and *Jesus* heard a voice addressed specifically to him: "*You* are my Son." No one else is in view here. Not the crowds of people—who aren't even mentioned—and not even John the Baptist. This is a moment of intimate revelation for Jesus, not a public announcement to all the world. And Mark lets you witness it.

This is a crucial part of Mark's message: you, the reader, are in on a secret that no one else in his Gospel seems to grasp. You know for certain that Jesus is the Son of God and that he bears God's seal of approval. In fact, as we read through this Gospel, we'll see Mark telling us how careful Jesus is not to let anyone around him know his true identity. *But you do.*

Driven Immediately

Mark next makes a quick pivot:

> The Spirit immediately drove him out into the wilderness. He was in the wilderness forty days, tempted by Satan; and he was with the wild beasts; and the angels waited on him. (1:12-13)

Immediately. Not a second passes between Jesus' baptism and his temptation in the wilderness. That moment of intimacy with God that Jesus enjoys is broken, and the revelation we receive is set aside, as Jesus is "driven" by the Spirit into the desert.

It might seem as if Mark is giving us no time to savor Jesus' experience of the Spirit or to ponder the meaning of God's words to his Son. But with a little Old Testament background, we can see that Mark is telling us something important about the ministry Jesus is about to undertake.

Driven. By telling us that the Spirit drove Jesus into the desert, Mark is pointing back to the holiest day in the Jewish calendar: the Day of Atonement, when the high priest entered the Holy of Holies in the Temple and made atonement for all the people's sins. (You can read about the rite of atonement in Leviticus 16.)

At one point during the rite, the high priest would bring out a goat before the people, lay his hands on the goat, and confess over it "all the iniquities of the people of Israel" (Leviticus 16:21). Then the goat—what we now call the scapegoat—would be driven into the desert, taking the people's sins with it. It's an elaborate ritual in which the people would clear a path and strike the goat with tree branches and throw stones at it as it went out to the wilderness.

Try to imagine this scene. Jesus had just been plunged into the Jordan River—the same river that "people from the whole Judean countryside and all the people of Jerusalem" had come to for cleansing (Mark 1:5). They came to be washed clean of their sins, and the waters of the Jordan accepted their offering. Then came Jesus. When he plunged into the water, all the sins that had accumulated there clung to him. All the impurities and iniquities of his fellow Jews came upon him. At that moment, he became "the Lamb of God who takes away the sin of the world" (John 1:29). As they were on the sacrificial goat, our sins were placed on Jesus, and he bore them into the desert.

Here at the very start, Mark is telling us something that everyone in his Gospel struggles to recognize: not only is Jesus the Son of God, but central to his life as God's Son is his humble acceptance of our sins. This isn't a Son of God who flaunts his power or lords it over his Father's creation. This isn't a Son who demands our subservience or who stands above his people.

No, Jesus' sonship is all about service, humility, and self-giving. It's about offering himself in sacrifice so that we—sinners though we are—can be reconciled with God and released from all of our sin and guilt.

For Reflection

1. Try to picture Jesus coming up out of the water after being baptized. Consider the expression on his face at this moment when he hears God's words of affirmation. How do you think he looks? Joyful? Puzzled? Worried? Why do you think he looks that way?

2. "With you I am well pleased" (Mark 1:11). Why do you think God the Father was so pleased with Jesus at this moment?

3. How does the driving-out ritual of the Day of Atonement help us understand Jesus' role? Aside from the crucifixion, can you think of another time in Jesus' life when he was treated the same way that the scapegoat was treated?

4. How does it feel when you hear about Jesus taking on the role of the scapegoat for you?

Repent and Believe, Part 1

Mark 1:14-45

"The time is fulfilled, and the kingdom of God has come near; repent, and believe in the good news."
(Mark 1:15)

Okay, the preliminaries are over. Mark has introduced us to Jesus, the Messiah and Son of God. Now he moves forward to show us Jesus' public ministry. And what a demonstration! Jesus is constantly on the move, exciting the crowds, agitating the religious leaders, and challenging his closest disciples.

Today's passage sets the pace: In a few short verses, Jesus announces his mission, calls his first disciples, casts out a demon, heals Peter's mother-in-law, spends the whole night healing people, gets up early to pray, and then heals a man with leprosy. All in about twenty-four hours.

By my count, this section is 607 words long—but only 95 of those words come from Jesus. That's only about 16 percent of the text. Not only that, but Jesus tends to speak in short, staccato phrases: "Be silent, and come out of him!" "I do choose. Be made clean!" (1:25, 41). Rather than focusing our attention on Jesus' teaching in his opening chapter, Mark keeps our gaze fixed firmly on what Jesus does—and he does a lot.

But there is one place where Jesus says a little more than this: at the very beginning. "The time is fulfilled," he proclaims, "and the kingdom of God has come near; repent, and believe in the good news" (1:15).

Repent and Believe

It seems simple enough. Just confess your sins and proclaim your faith in God. But look at what comes after Jesus' announcement. Or rather, look at what *doesn't* come after it. Nowhere in these opening stories do we see anyone repenting in the traditional sense of admitting their guilt or confessing their sins. In fact, the first time that Mark even mentions sin is a few days after these events, *after* he has finished preaching in the towns surrounding Capernaum (2:5).

I can't impress upon you enough how important this is. Mark is telling us something we can easily miss if our understanding of repentance is restricted to begging God to pardon our sinfulness. The Greek word Mark uses for "repent" is *metanoia*. The word means "to change one's mind" or to think in a new way or redirect one's heart.

It's as if Jesus is saying, *The time for the kingdom has come, and you'll miss it if you don't change your way of thinking. So do it! Change your mind; change your assumptions [repent]; and welcome this new thing with open arms [believe].*

What are we to change our minds about? Mark doesn't tell us directly, but he uses the stories of healings and exorcisms in the next few chapters to show us. We get a glimpse of them here, and a more obvious one will come in the next chapter. For now, let's look at just one story: the disciples' early-morning interaction with Jesus.

That Is What I Came Out to Do

We've already seen Simon, Andrew, James, and John leave their nets to follow Jesus. He has promised they will fish for people, and in these opening scenes, plenty of people seem to have entered their nets: the whole town of Capernaum shows up that evening looking for healing. Everyone wants a piece of Jesus, and he willingly obliges. He works miracles long into the night. But when morning comes, he is nowhere to be found.

This is where this scene opens. The disciples pursue Jesus and find him in a deserted place, praying. They try to persuade him to come back, but Jesus refuses. He doesn't want a repeat of the night before; he wants to move on to the towns surrounding Capernaum "so that I may proclaim the message there also" (Mark 1:38).

The disciples were looking for more miracles and more crowds, but Jesus was looking for changed hearts and minds. This was his primary mission. So Jesus redirects their thinking. He helps them repent—change their minds—so that they can focus on the good news he is proclaiming.

This is the first of many times that Mark will portray the disciples as misunderstanding Jesus' mission, and I believe he includes these little scenes for a reason. He's not interested in telling us how slow to believe the disciples were as much as he is in asking us what we believe. And that's where I want to end this chapter. Jesus came out to do something, and he asked us to take on a new attitude and a new way of thinking in order to receive it. We'll spend the next few days examining this new way of thinking more closely, but for now let's get ourselves in the right frame of mind. You can use the following questions in prayer today to help you get ready.

For Reflection

1. How would you describe the "good news" that you believe? Spend a few minutes writing out your understanding of Jesus' gospel message. See if you can boil it down to two or three sentences—and be careful not to use pat phrases like "Just love people" or "Place your faith in Christ."

2. When Jesus called Simon and Andrew to follow him, he promised they would end up fishing for people. What kind of "fishing" do you think they were expecting to do? How were their expectations different from—or similar to—Jesus' expectations?

3. Do you think Jesus is asking you to "catch" certain people in your life in the net of his good news? As you read the next few chapters, see if God suggests to you a humble, winning approach to help them encounter Jesus.

4. Imagine that you are one of the disciples who found Jesus early in the morning. You are about to urge him to come back into town to be with the people, but you notice he is praying. What does that scene look like to you? What is the expression on Jesus' face as he prays? Look at him for a moment before speaking to him. What do you want to say to him now?

Repent and Believe, Part 2

Mark 2:1–3:6

"Son, your sins are forgiven." (Mark 2:5)

Yesterday, we saw that Jesus' call, "Repent, and believe in the good news" (Mark 1:15), seemed out of place because it wasn't followed by accounts of people actually repenting. Well, that changes with the stories we're going to read today. But they're not the accounts of repentance you might expect.

Perhaps the most striking of these is the account of the paralyzed man in Mark 2:1-12. It's a familiar enough story— Jesus is at home speaking to such a large crowd that the paralyzed man's friends can't get in the door. They resort to ripping up the roof in order to get to Jesus. Mark tells us that Jesus "saw their faith" and proclaimed that the man's sins were forgiven (2:5). There's a second half to this story—the reaction of the scribes to Jesus' healing of the man's paralysis. But let's stick with the first half at this point.

What I find so intriguing about this story is the way Mark intertwines Jesus' call to repentance and belief. Whereas we might consider it to be a two-step process, Mark shows us that they are two ways of saying the same thing: you can't repent without believing, and you can't believe without repenting.

Embedded Repentance

Mark makes it clear that Jesus is responding to the *faith* that the man's friends showed. Their faith was strong enough that it convinced them to push through every obstacle: the crowd at the door, the barrier of the roof, even the logistics of hoisting their friend up to the roof and lowering him down without letting him tumble to the ground. Over and over in Mark's Gospel, we'll meet people who show this kind of faith. They are the true heroes of his story, and it's for good reason that they stand out in our memories.

So on one level, there's the "believe" part of repent and believe. These friends show the kind of faith that Jesus was looking for, and that's why he responded to them so generously.

But where's the repentance? On the surface, it doesn't seem to be there at all. Jesus simply saw the friends' faith and declared the man's sins to be forgiven. Nobody cried out, "Lord, have mercy on me!" or "Leave me, Lord, for I am a sinner!"

In fact, the repentance was there all along. It was embedded in the friends' acts of faith. By acting as persistently and trustingly as they did, they demonstrated the kind of change of heart and mind that Jesus was looking for.

First, there was a change *from* selfishness *to* selflessness. The man's friends didn't seek anything for themselves. They were concerned first and foremost for their friend whose life had been limited so dramatically. Their commitment to him reflected a radical kind of love of neighbor—especially the poor and needy—that always moves Jesus' heart.

Second, there was a change *from* resignation *to* hope. These friends had confidence in Jesus' power to heal. And that confidence motivated them to overcome all the roadblocks facing them. Without this confidence, they would have been far more likely to give up at the first sign of difficulty and let their friend resign himself to a life of suffering.

Do you see how repentance is behind all of this? Remember what we discussed yesterday, that the word for repentance—*metanoia*—means a change of mind and heart. To make such a change requires leaving behind one set of attitudes and assumptions and adopting a different set of attitudes and assumptions.

What about Sin?

The question might arise: what about sin? Doesn't focusing on a change of heart and mind minimize the impact of our specific acts of disobedience to God's commandments? Not exactly. Every sin we commit is serious. It's an affront to the holiness of God, and it leaves us vulnerable to greater and more painful sins. And of course, it's sin that separates us from God and casts a shadow over our ability to live in love.

But the testimony of Scripture is clear that the only way to overcome sin is through a kind of repentance that goes beyond seeking pardon. From the story of Cain and Abel, when God warned Cain that sin is "lurking at the door" (Genesis 4:7), to St. Paul's urging that we "be transformed *by the renewing of [our] minds*" (Romans 12:2, emphasis added), God is constantly asking us to change the way we think. He is constantly asking us to repent of our old ways of thinking and believe the good news that Jesus announced. Because it really is good news, and it can change our entire life.

Where's the Good News?

By now you may be wondering, *Okay, you've been talking a lot about repentance, and I get it. But what is the good news Jesus is asking us to believe?* That's a fair question, and I'm going to ask you to have just a little more patience. We'll get there in a couple of days. In fact, there is much more I'd love to say right now, but I'm running out of space, and you're running out of time. Instead, take a look at the following questions, some of which touch on other stories from Mark in this section, and see if you sense God opening your heart more to his message.

For Reflection

1. Each of the stories in this section offers a different window into Jesus' call to repent and believe. Take a look at one of them, and see if you can discover the kind of repentance that Jesus is calling for. What change of heart and mind does he want his hearers to undergo? What is he asking them to believe that is different from what they already hold to be true?

2. Mark often embeds opposites in his stories. There is the faith of the paralyzed man's friends contrasted with the hard hearts of some scribes. There's Jesus graciously joining Levi at dinner contrasted with the grumbling of some of the "scribes of the Pharisees" (2:16). And there's the freedom of the apostles picking grain on the Sabbath contrasted with the rule-bound attitude of some Pharisees (see 2:23-24). Mark uses these opposites to demonstrate the tension between Jesus and some of the religious leaders. But he also uses them to prompt us to examine where we stand on the continuum between these contrasts. To what degree, for instance, do you feel like the disciples enjoying dinner with "sinners" such as Levi's friends, and how much do you feel like the Pharisees who grumbled at such social and religious mingling?

3. Imagine that you are the man suffering from paralysis in today's first story. What thoughts go through your mind as this story unfolds? What kind of repentance (change of mind and heart) do you think Jesus is asking you—the recipient of this miracle—to make?

4. Finally, spend some time letting Jesus' words—*Repent, and believe in the good news*—resonate in your heart. Listen to him saying it over and over again. What does his voice sound like? Is there a particular area of your heart that he is asking you to examine and change? As you sit with Jesus, see if anything comes to mind that you might need to take to the Sacrament of Reconciliation. But remember, repentance is about asking God to help you change the attitudes and assumptions that keep you from experiencing his love. It isn't only about confessing what you have done or failed to do.

Inside and Outside

Mark 3:7-35

He went up the mountain and called to him those
whom he wanted, and they came to him.
(Mark 3:13)

It's not uncommon among those who know a few things
about the Bible to pay less attention to Mark's Gospel than to the other three. It could be because Mark's is
the shortest, so they think that the others go into greater
depth. They may think that since Mark's is the first, it is
a kind of rough draft that the others improved upon. It
could also be because Mark's Greek can be a bit rough
at times, especially compared with the poetic beauty of

Matthew's Sermon on the Mount or the opening chapter of John's Gospel.

But Mark is a genius—and not only because he pioneered the idea of writing a Gospel. He is also surprisingly strategic in the way he tells his story. Today's passage gives us two examples of just how strategic Mark can be. They also show how effective these strategies are in helping us to see Jesus—and ourselves—in a new light.

A Large Crowd, Some Disciples, the Twelve

First, look at how Mark tells the story of Jesus choosing his twelve apostles. He begins by talking about "a great multitude" that follows Jesus to the Sea of Galilee (3:7). Mark shows us an unruly crowd—so much so that Jesus needed to have a boat ready "so that they would not crush him" (3:9). This was no polite group of religious people, such as you might see lining up for Communion at Mass.

After spending some time with this crowd, Jesus leaves and goes up a mountain where he "called to him those whom he wanted" (3:13). Not everyone is invited—only a small, hand-picked group of followers. And it's from among this group that Jesus chooses an even smaller cohort: the Twelve who would become his apostles.

I want you to see how purposeful Mark is here. As he has done before, and as he will do in the coming verses, Mark is highlighting the difference between those who come to Jesus looking for something and those who come in response to a personal call from him. The former aren't necessarily embracing Jesus and his teachings, but the latter clearly are. Mark is asking us which group we belong to—and which group we want to belong to.

Outside vs. Inside

Immediately after this, Mark repeats the same pattern, only in a more pointed and more personal manner. First, there's the crowd again, and they're as demanding as ever—Jesus and his disciples "could not even eat" (3:20). Then comes Jesus' family, who has heard rumors that "he has gone out of his mind." They seem to believe this, for they set out "to restrain him" (3:21). Then scribes from Jerusalem appear, accusing Jesus of being in league with Beelzebul, "the ruler of the demons" (3:22).

That's quite a pileup of opposition, misunderstanding, and menace![1] And what does Jesus do in response to it all? Once more, he calls a smaller group together and teaches them.

Again, Mark structures the scene masterfully. The crowd, Jesus' family, and the scribes remain standing outside the house, distant from Jesus. They may be trying to get to him, but not because of faith. Rather than listen to Jesus, they interrupt him and disrupt his ministry. By contrast, a smaller group of people are inside the house, sitting around Jesus and listening to his teaching. These are the ones he has called to be with him, and they have answered the call. Again, almost unavoidably, the question arises: *Where am I? Inside or outside? Sitting at Jesus' feet or standing apart from him?*

An Invitation for You

Well, imagine you are inside, sitting with Jesus. Here he is, a compelling spiritual teacher and powerful worker of wonders—and he is choosing to spend time with *you*! Think of what he is putting aside in order to be with you: the limelight offered by the clamoring crowd. The approval of Jerusalem's religious elite. Even the closeness of his own family. In fact, he considers you part of his true family: you are one who "does the will of God," and that's all he is looking for (3:35). A humble, eager desire to follow the Lord and to be pleasing to him. A readiness to hear his call and a willingness to respond to it.

For Reflection

1. Think about times in the day when you find yourself on the outside and feel distant from Jesus. Can you identify with any of the groups in today's passage who were similarly on the outside? Perhaps you focused too much on what you wanted Jesus to do for you. Maybe you took your relationship with him for granted. Or maybe you got too caught up in what you were doing and forgot about him. How can you get back to being close to him? Or to put it another way, how can you "repent, and believe in the good news" (1:15)?

2. Are there times when you wonder if Jesus is "out of his mind" (Mark 3:21)? Perhaps you feel that he is too demanding or too hard to understand. Have you ever thought of telling Jesus what you think? How do you imagine he would respond?

3. Jesus will have more to say to you later, and he will do it in the form of parables. But for today, just let his words sink in: you are his mother, his brother, his sister. Jesus treasures you; he values your desire to be with him. There may be challenges to come. There may be persecution or misunderstanding, just as he experienced. But for today, place yourself in that small group inside the house. Sit at his feet and listen for whatever he wants to tell you.

The Kingdom in Parables

Mark 4:1-41

"To you has been given the secret of the kingdom of God." (Mark 4:11)

Finally! After three chapters, we are getting some of Jesus' actual teachings. Yes, he said a few things about Satan driving out Satan, but that was in response to outsiders' accusations. But here, Jesus isn't prompted by any conflict or challenge. His teaching comes on his own initiative. And just what is this teaching? The all-familiar parable of the sower and the seed.

Now, I'm going to ask you to do something: read the parable *and only the parable*. Just stick with Mark 4:3-8. It's a bit strange, don't you think? A sower throws his seed everywhere, with predictable results. Of course the seeds that end up in inhospitable environments won't do well. Naturally the ones that land in good soil will take root and bear fruit. *Why,* you may wonder, *is Jesus telling this story? Not only is it an obvious observation, but I don't see how it relates to all he has done so far.*

Clearly, Jesus is after more than best agricultural practices. But he doesn't say exactly *what* he is after. Immediately afterward, we find him surrounded once more by that smaller group of disciples made up of the twelve apostles and some other followers. They're the ones who get to hear the explanation.

Looking, but Not Seeing

Here again we have a contrast between the crowd and the disciples, those on the outside and those on the inside. Jesus even admits to it openly: "To you has been given the secret of the kingdom of God, but for those outside, everything comes in parables" (4:11). Why would he do this?

Because Jesus knows the crowd for what it is. He has had numerous interactions with these people by now, and he sees that they look but can't perceive anything beyond his status as a wonder-worker. They may hear him teach, but they don't understand his call to repent and believe in the good news (see 4:12). All he can give them are short, intriguing stories in the hopes of arousing their curiosity and compelling them to look for more than miracles and exorcisms.

But Jesus has a different view of his disciples. They are more open to him. They have responded to his call to repent and believe. They are more likely to grasp his message and become his messengers. So he speaks to them in plain language.

Still, even this group falls short. "Do you not understand this parable?" he asks them. "Then how will you understand all the parables?" (4:13).

Teaching by Doing

I don't want to dive too deeply into Jesus' explanation. It's pretty obvious, after all: pay attention to Jesus, and you'll end up living a fruitful, fulfilled life. But if you focus on the lies of the devil or the hardships and anxieties of life, your relationship with God will wither. Makes sense, right?

Instead, I want to focus on Jesus' first response to his disciples. He seems surprised that they have to ask him to explain the parables to them. "To you has been given the secret of the kingdom of God," he tells them (4:11). He makes it sound as if this is something they should already know—that they should already understand what his parable of the sower and the seed means.

You might forgive the disciples if they feel a little frustrated at this point. What is there to understand if Jesus hasn't done much in the way of formal teaching yet? But perhaps Jesus has been teaching them all along—not by way of sermons as much as by way of his actions. Let's take a quick look back:

- He demonstrated his authority over demons—Mark 1:21-28.
- He demonstrated his authority over sin—Mark 2:1-12.
- He demonstrated a special concern for those whose sin had made them outcasts—Mark 2:15-17.
- He demonstrated his authority over the Law of Moses— Mark 2:23-28.
- He demonstrated his mission to form a new family, a new community centered on his teaching—Mark 3:13-19, 31-35.

Signs of the Kingdom

At this point, you might be tempted to think that Jesus has been using these events to tell his disciples that he is the Son of God and therefore deserving of their obedience and submission. But I don't think that's what's going on here. Remember, Jesus has also commanded demons *not* to call him by that title (see 3:11-12), and he has forbidden people to spread word of his ability to perform miracles (see 1:44). Jesus wants to keep his identity a secret, at least for now.

So let me take you back to something we'll be revisiting over and over: Jesus' foundational call to repent and believe. Jesus isn't giving away the whole story yet, but he is asking people to change their hearts and minds and put their faith in something he calls the gospel, or the "good news." A couple of days ago, I said we couldn't exactly put our finger on what Jesus means when he speaks of this good news. But now we just may have enough stories of Jesus in action to help us come to an early answer—and, not surprisingly, it's been hiding in plain sight all along.

So what is the good news? Exactly what Jesus announced at the beginning: "The time is fulfilled, and the kingdom of God has come near" (1:15). Everything Jesus has done—all the people he has healed, all the demons he has cast out, all the sinners he has welcomed, all the wisdom he has shown—these are all signs that a new era has dawned. They are signs that the kingdom of God truly is at hand and that God is making good on the promises he made through Moses and the prophets.

Something new is on the horizon, and only those who change their hearts and minds will be able to see it and receive it. They are the ones on the inside, the ones who, like the good soil in the parable, hear God's word and accept it with open, humble hearts.

For Everyone

It's all so wonderful. And when you look at what Jesus has said and done so far, it seems obvious as well. But despite all the evidence, the disciples can't see it. They ask Jesus to explain something he thinks they should be able to understand on their own. We'll see this even more clearly tomorrow, but for today, let's focus on the main point of Jesus' parable: everyone who listens to him and believes in his teachings *will bear fruit*. The kingdom of God is here for *everyone* who will repent and believe.

For Reflection

1. The chapter ends with the story of the disciples panicking during a storm at sea while Jesus is fast asleep in their boat. When they wake him up, Jesus rebukes the waves and asks them a pointed question: "Have you still no faith?" (4:40). After all they have seen Jesus do and heard him say, they remain confused and fearful. Do you think Jesus is too harsh in his rebuke of the disciples? Or is he justified in calling them out?

2. Spend some time today meditating on Jesus' explanation of the parable of the sower and the seed. Where do you see examples of "bad soil" in your life—the temptations of the evil one, shallow roots in Jesus' teachings, and too great a focus on the cares and anxieties of life? But don't limit yourself to the negative questions. Look also for where and how the seeds of God's word have been sown in your life. Look in the usual places, like Mass, the sacraments, or times of prayer. But look also at areas like work, family, friendships, even struggles and setbacks.

3. After looking at the soil of your life and the seed that God has sown, ask God if there is one area of your life—a habit, perhaps, or an attitude, or a relationship—in which he is inviting you to take another step closer to him. Or to put it in Mark's terms, how is Jesus asking you to repent and believe in the good news today?

Delivered from Evil

Mark 5:1-20

They came to Jesus and saw the demoniac sitting there, clothed and in his right mind. (Mark 5:15)

If anyone tries to tell you that the field of psychology began in the late nineteenth century with Sigmund Freud, ask them to read this story. Here, in a few short paragraphs, Mark gives us a profound and insightful anatomy of the human mind and its relationship with sin, evil, and God. Let's take a look.

Trapped in a Vicious Cycle

The poor fellow! We don't know how he came to be possessed by all those demons, and in one sense, it doesn't matter. What matters is the way these evil spirits tormented him. They pushed him to acts of self-harm. They drove him into a deathlike isolation in a graveyard. And they gave him a superhuman strength that was as terrifying as it was uncontrollable. Everyone who had once been close to him had given up on him and pretty much left him for dead.

Here is a man drenched in torment and misery, yet he rebuffs every attempt to help him. He hates what he has become, yet he cannot bring himself to be anything else. His existence is a kind of living death, with no sign of relief or release.

In a similar way, we all have some experience of the vicious cycle that sin can produce. Whether it is the kind of insecure pride that constantly needs praise or a misguided sense of self-sufficiency that alienates us from loved ones or a fixation on possessions that breeds envy and covetousness, each of us has had the experience of being ensnared in sin. If we look closely enough, we could probably also recognize the lies the devil has whispered to us in order to keep us there. But there is hope, and Mark portrays its dawning in dramatic fashion.

Restored to Peace

The moment Jesus steps into this man's bleak existence, an inner conflict arises that is by turns filled with hope and crushing in its despair. The man bows before Jesus in a gesture of worship and submission, but he can bring himself only to curse him and try to drive him away. He openly admits how tormenting his inner conflict is. He wants to be set free, but he is terrified at the thought of living without his demons. He hates them, but he doesn't want them to go. They have so taken over his life that he can't imagine how he could live any other way.

This story is so intense that you might have a hard time relating to it. But try this thought experiment. Think of the last time you went to Confession. You knew there were sins you needed to confess. You knew these sins were causing damage, whether to your relationships with your loved ones, to your relationship with God, or to your own heart. Part of you wanted to come clean and experience the freedom that comes with absolution. But at the same time, you didn't want to go. You knew it would be hard to speak your sins out loud—even if you had chosen the anonymity of confessing behind the screen—so you tried to rationalize your way out of the sacrament.

Now, you weren't possessed as this man was, but you were experiencing a similar kind of conflict. You were feeling the tug-of-war between the lies of the devil and the yearnings of your conscience. The evil one tried to convince you that Jesus was a threat rather than a savior—a tormentor rather than a comforter. He also tried to convince you that you'd be better off resigning yourself to sin instead of going through the embarrassment of confessing it. But somehow you persevered and entered the confessional.

It felt uncomfortable in there at first, didn't it? You still weren't sure how things were going to unfold. But you pushed through the resistance and confessed. And as you did, you realized that it wasn't so bad after all. The priest likely treated you with respect and understanding as he offered words of guidance and encouragement. In the span of just a few minutes, all the turmoil of your inner conflict was driven away, and you were left with a sense of peace. Maybe a little more humility as well. In the end, you felt like the man in today's story: sitting quietly, clothed with dignity, and in your right mind once more.

Delivered and Commissioned

This story follows Mark's account of the storm at sea. In that earlier story, we saw the power that Jesus has over the elements of nature. We also saw how little faith the disciples had, even after all they had seen and heard. In today's story we see how much power Jesus has over the supernatural elements that sin has unleashed into the world. He routs, not just one, but an entire legion of demons by the power of his word, and a man once trapped and tormented is now at peace. Back-to-back, we have two stories that show us how absolute and encompassing Jesus' power is. No storm— whether literal or figurative, whether "out there" or in the depth of our hearts—can withstand him. That means that we are safe when we place ourselves in his hands.

I started off by talking about Mark's grasp of human psychology, and I hope my few comments have shown how deep his insights are. He takes this story of Jesus' encounter with a demoniac and uses it as an external model of every person's internal conflict. He takes all of the inner, hidden details of our struggle with sin and uses this man's torment to uncover them and magnify them. And as he does, he shows us that someone who is about as outside of God's grace as possible can be brought inside. No one is too far gone— Jesus can rescue anyone.

For Reflection

1. Why do you think Jesus sent the man into the Decapolis to preach? Why do you think he was so quick to send him out instead of insisting that he join Peter and the others as a disciple?

2. By accepting Jesus' command to go out and announce his deliverance, this man, once the ultimate outsider, demonstrates a faith that the disciples, those most on the inside, do not demonstrate. Do you doubt that certain people you know would ever come to believe in Christ? What kind of hope does this man's story give you when you think of them?

3. Place yourself in the shoes of one of Jesus' disciples, and replay this scene in your imagination. You have just seen Jesus calm a storm at sea, and you have just heard him question the depth of your faith. With these two events fresh in your mind, you see him not only deliver a demoniac but send him out to proclaim the good news of his deliverance. Imagine how Jesus might answer you if you were to ask him to explain what just happened.

Outsiders Brought Inside

Mark 5:21-43

"Your faith has made you well." (Mark 5:34)

The crowd is at it again. This time, they show up, not once, but twice. First, they are jostling Jesus as he tries to make his way to Jairus' house. Then another kind of crowd appears outside of Jairus' house, wailing at the news of his daughter's death. Will they never let up?

You may wonder why I keep going on about the crowds. All I can do right now is ask you to keep track of them and to pay attention to the way Mark compares and contrasts them with other characters in his stories. As you do, a clearer picture will emerge.

A Real Outsider

The last time we saw a crowd, Jesus was delivering his parable of the sower and the seed. Both Mark and Jesus himself were quite explicit that this group did not merit to hear the meaning behind Jesus' parables. In the story of the hemorrhaging woman, we see something even more sad: no matter how close they get to Jesus, the people who make up the crowd don't seem to know who he is—and so they miss out on his grace and his power to heal. Only one person has the faith for that, and she stands apart from the crowd. She is an outsider.

Actually, this woman is an outsider two times over. First, there's her gender. Women were considered second- or third-class citizens in the patriarchal culture of first-century Palestine. Add to that the fact that Jesus is a single man, and you can imagine that people might have interpreted her touching Jesus' cloak as an act of shameless norm breaking more than as an act of faith. So there's the first level of exclusion.

But there's also her religious status. This woman's ailment would have rendered her ritually unclean. The Law of Moses states that any woman who has "a discharge of blood for many days, not at the time of her impurity, . . . shall continue in uncleanness" (Leviticus 15:25). But what does that entail? For one thing, she would be barred from the Temple in Jerusalem. But on a more practical level,

> Every bed on which she lies during all the days of her discharge shall be treated as the bed of her impurity; and

everything on which she sits shall be unclean, as in the uncleanness of her impurity. Whoever touches these things shall be unclean, and shall wash his clothes, and bathe in water, and be unclean until the evening. (15:26-27)

So this woman would have had to live in extreme isolation. Her contact with her husband and family would have been strictly curtailed. Her relationships with the other women in her village would have been strained at best, maybe even hostile. She was about as far outside as you could get.

Here is where the real miracle of this woman's story lies. According to the popular piety of the day, people cut off like this didn't generally receive special favors from God. In fact, she could have suffered censure from the authorities for "contaminating" a rabbi by daring to touch his cloak. But what does Jesus do? He heals her! He calls her "daughter" (Mark 5:34). He welcomes her as part of the new family he is creating (see 3:31-35). She moves to the head of the line, bypassing the noisy, faithless crowd as well as Jesus' disciples.

Do Not Fear, Only Believe

Much of what we saw in the story of the hemorrhaging woman is also evident in the story of Jairus' daughter:

- There's a crowd that seems oblivious to Jesus and his power to heal. Mark makes it clear that Jesus "put them all outside" before going to heal the girl (5:40).

- There's impurity spread by human touch: Jewish law forbade people other than close family to touch a corpse, but Jesus took this little girl by the hand.
- There's the breaking of social norms: As a leader in his synagogue, Jairus should not have been bowing down to Jesus, let alone begging him to come to his home.
- There's Jesus' radical act of welcoming someone considered beyond acceptable: His words to the dead child, *Talitha cum,* are words of affection and closeness (5:41). Another translation, in fact, would be "Little lamb, stand up"—a statement that reflects the intimacy of the moment.

So once more, outsiders are brought inside—but not just because they are outsiders. Their faith plays an important role. Jesus told the woman, "Daughter, your faith has made you well" (5:34). And he told Jairus, "Do not fear, only believe" (5:36). As I've mentioned previously, the true heroes in Mark's Gospel are the outsiders, not the disciples. They're the ones who, like Jairus and this woman, accept Jesus' invitation, "Repent, and believe in the good news" (1:15).

Repent and Believe

Where do you see repentance? For the hemorrhaging woman, you see it as she sheds the restrictions of the purity code that has kept her isolated for years. She changes her mind about what the Law says about her condition—and, by extension, about her. Further, she "repents" by changing her mind about the restrictions put on her because she is a woman. Believing in the good news about Jesus' power and his mercy, she finds the boldness to reach out to him. Believing in the good news that Jesus is willing to heal her, she risks censure and condemnation. And because she has believed, she is not only healed but also made a daughter in the family of God.

As for Jairus, the repentance comes as he puts aside the same purity code that would have kept Jesus from laying hands on his daughter. He has spent years upholding that code in his synagogue, but none of that matters for him now that it is his own *Talitha,* his little lamb, whose life was on the line. He also repents when he prostrates himself before Jesus and begs him "repeatedly" on behalf of his daughter (5:23). He steps out of the cultural and social restrictions that would have placed Jesus below him in status. Advocating for his daughter, he places his faith in Jesus—a man whose words and deeds have put him at odds with the religious system to which Jairus has dedicated his life.

Opposite Poles, One Faith

Taken together, Jairus and the hemorrhaging woman show us that being on the inside or the outside isn't a matter of social standing—it's a matter of faith and humility. These two people occupy opposite poles on the spectrum of religious purity and acceptability, yet both are welcomed by Jesus. Their faith brings them closer to Jesus than the crowd could ever experience—closer, even, than his disciples. It makes them part of his family.

For Reflection

1. According to the French scholar of religion René Girard,[2] Christianity stands apart from all other religions in its opposition to purity codes and insider-outsider distinctions. At the center of our faith is a person, Jesus, who was treated as the ultimate outsider and who welcomed those who were on the outside. His resurrection, according to Girard, showed that God himself stands on the outside, in solidarity with the victims of prejudice, abuse, and social structures. The stories of Jairus' daughter and the hemorrhaging woman show this preference for the lowly and marginalized. Can you think of another story about Jesus that also illustrates this principle?

2. "You see the crowd pressing in on you; how can you say, 'Who touched me?'" (Mark 5:31). With these words, Jesus' disciples show their own lack of faith. With their eyes fixed on the crowd and its pushy attitude, they are oblivious to the woman's act of faith—and to the healing power she has experienced. What is it about crowds that drains people's faith?

3. Compare the story of the healing of Jairus' daughter with the story of the raising of Lazarus in the Gospel of John, chapter 11. Where do you see a crowd in both stories? How does Jesus respond to them? What kind of faith does he ask of Jairus and of Martha and Mary?

Are they different? Or is Jesus saying the same thing, only in a different way?

The Ultimate Outsider

Mark 6:1-13

Many who heard him were astounded. (Mark 6:2)

We just saw how two outsiders—the woman with a hemorrhage and Jairus, the synagogue leader—became insiders, people who show faith in Jesus. We also saw how people in close proximity to Jesus—the crowd, for instance—can still be so far on the outside that they fail to experience his power to heal or save. As we have seen over and over again, plenty of people end up spiritually distant from Jesus. Even his disciples. Even his family.

Now as we look at Jesus' visit to his hometown of Nazareth, we see another inside/outside dynamic. But this time, the script is flipped.

Astounded and Scandalized

Jesus arrives home, and as you might expect, he is invited to preach in the synagogue where he grew up. Most likely, news of his miracles and other spiritual exploits has preceded his arrival, so you can imagine Nazarenes being eager to see a local boy who has made a name for himself in the big city of Capernaum.

At the same time, you can also imagine his family coming to the synagogue with some degree of anxiety. Surely they would have remembered their last encounter with him, when they were concerned that Jesus might be going "out of his mind" (Mark 3:21). They would have remembered his rebuke when he said that his true mother and brothers and sisters were those who did God's will. That scene surely didn't assuage their concerns—and neither would this episode.

Mark tells us that the people gathered at the synagogue were "astounded" by Jesus' teaching and wondered aloud where Jesus got all of his "wisdom" (6:2). We can read this in a generous way, as in the people were amazed, excited, thrilled to hear all that he had to say. But the Greek word Mark used (*exeplessonto*) can just as easily be translated as shocked, alarmed, or even aghast.

Considering how this episode unfolds, I think the second translation is more appropriate. For in the next line, Mark says that the people "took offense" at Jesus (6:3). Again, a little Greek is helpful here. The word Mark uses is *eskandalizonto*, a word whose root gives us "scandalize" in English. To make matters worse, Jesus was unable to perform many healings or do much to help them. All because they were so offended and scandalized by him and his teaching.

We don't know what Jesus said to have shocked and scandalized the people, but we might find some clues in this passage as well as in some of his earlier teachings and sayings. Let me make a few suggestions.

Family, Faith, and Prophecy

First, it's possible that Jesus felt compelled to expound on his earlier message to his family: "Whoever does the will of God is my brother and sister and mother" (Mark 3:35). He could have spoken about what it means to be a member of the family of God: that his Father did not play favorites or overlook people's sins because of their relationship to him. He could have expounded on his call to repent and believe the good news—that repentance included turning away from attitudes of elitism or exclusion. Perhaps too he spoke about the need to be open to *anyone* who loves God and is trying to follow the commandments.

Second, it's possible that Jesus anticipated the people's lack of openness to him by talking about the centrality of faith—a living faith—for anyone who wanted to experience God's healing touch. We read at the end of this account that Jesus "was amazed *at their unbelief*," so it's possible that faith was at the heart of his message (6:6, emphasis added). Again, as in the first possibility, Jesus may have spoken about the people's need to make a personal decision to follow him and not rely on their familial bonds with him or on any other inside track they might think they had.

Third, if we take a hint from Jesus' words about a prophet not being accepted among his own people, we might imagine that he spoke about the prophets of Israel and how he falls in line with those great heroes of the past. Ominously, the inference here would be that the fate of the prophets would be his fate: rejection and persecution by his own people.

The Ultimate Outsider

Whatever Jesus said, the message was challenging enough to scandalize the people. It was inclusive enough to threaten their assumption of special status. Ultimately, it was demanding enough that most of them were moved to reject him. And that rejection must have stung. These were his people, his family and friends. As a child, he played with them in the streets of the village. Some of them were trusted clients of his and Joseph's. The women would have been friends with Mary. And now they refused to accept him. They made him an outsider.

This is not the first time Jesus has experienced rejection. In fact, the image of Jesus as the outsider runs throughout Mark's Gospel:

- We see it immediately after Jesus' baptism, when the Spirit "drives" Jesus deeper into the wilderness—and farther away from the cities and towns of Israel (Mark 1:12).
- We see it after Jesus heals a man with leprosy. Having touched an unclean man, he himself is made unclean and so "could no longer go into a town openly, but stayed out in the country" (1:45).
- We see it after he performs a healing on the Sabbath and thus incurs the wrath of the Pharisees, who "went out and immediately conspired with the Herodians against him, how to destroy him" (3:6).
- We see it in the scribes' connecting him with Beelzebul, "the ruler of the demons" (3:22).
- We will see it even more dramatically as Jesus begins to make his way toward Jerusalem, as he predicts he will be "rejected by the elders, the chief priests, and the scribes, and be killed" (8:31).
- And finally, we will see his rejection reach its climax in his Passion, as he is "handed over" repeatedly until no one will accept him, and he is nailed to a cross (see 15:1, 10, 15).

But that is for the future. For now, Jesus must leave his hometown and continue on his mission. As the story continues, keep your eyes open for signs of Jesus' growing outsider status. Keep them open too for ways he invites other people to join him in accepting that status for themselves—and see their reaction. Finally, keep your own heart open to Jesus' invitation for you to join him on the outside.

For Reflection

1. What do you think Jesus said in the synagogue at Nazareth? What could he have said to make the people there reject him? Spend a little time imagining Jesus' teaching. If you have more time, write out your thoughts about his sermon on that day.

2. How do you think Jesus felt about being on the outside? Take one or more of the bullet points above, and think about how he must have felt as a result of his increasing isolation. How do you think his reaction changed over time as his outsider status became clearer and more menacing?

3. Where do you see people being isolated or excluded today? Why do you think they are being excluded, and who do you think is doing the excluding? What do you think Jesus would say, both to the excluders and the excluded? And finally, what do you want to say to each group?

4. Is there something about Jesus that scandalizes you? Something that makes you want to push him a little further away? Tell him about it in prayer, then quiet your heart and try to hear what he might want to say to you.

A Tale of Two Kings

Mark 6:14-56

He had compassion for them, because they were like sheep without a shepherd. (Mark 6:34)

It's an odd pairing: the death of John the Baptist, the greatest prophet, at the hands of a tyrant, followed by the story of the multiplication of the loaves. But I believe Mark put these stories together for a reason. Remember, the story about John's beheading is a flashback; Mark could have inserted it any number of places. But he chose this spot, and he might have done so in order to show the stark contrast between Herod, Israel's earthly ruler, and Jesus, the rightful king of the Jewish people.

Two Banquets

First, there's the contrast between the kind of banquet each king gives. Herod's order to execute John the Baptist takes place during a lavish dinner. He is hosting a birthday party in his own honor, and he is surrounded by important guests. You can imagine the menu: the finest cuts of lamb and veal, the creamiest hummus, juicy pomegranates, sweet figs, and the freshest fish direct from the Sea of Galilee. Of course there would be wine in abundance. All the signs of wealth and prosperity would have been present.

Jesus also hosts a banquet. But he's not honoring himself, and he has not surrounded himself with the elites of Galilee. Rather, he has gathered the lost and the poor, the ones who live "like sheep without a shepherd" because their leader, Herod, is too busy courting the rich (Mark 6:34). What's more, the people have not assembled to fawn over Jesus or play the power games that often accompany political banquets. They have come "from all the towns" because of Jesus' reputation as a healer and wonder-worker (6:33). They have come to receive healing, not to influence him.

As for the menu at Jesus' banquet: bread and fish. Not the fresh-out-of-the-oven bread that Herod would have provided, but whatever bread the disciples had left over from their recent missionary journey. And not fresh-caught fish, but the dried, preserved kind that a traveler would keep in reserve in case he couldn't find an inn or a friendly home to welcome him for the night. Not a very appetizing menu.

But there's something about this food that makes it valuable: *it was a miracle.* It was God's provision for a people stranded in a "deserted place" (6:35). Like the manna that miraculously appeared in another desert, it was a sign that God was close to his people in their need. It was a sign that even though they had been ignored and abused by their leaders (whether Pharaoh or Herod), God saw them and cared for them. The food was simple, yes, but its simplicity didn't take away from the divine love and compassion that brought it forth.

Finally, Jesus' banquet ends with all of his guests having eaten their fill—and with more left over. Not only that, but it also ends with his disciples having had the joy of working with him to help make the miracle happen. Everyone is filled up, both with food and with hope for their future.

Herod's banquet, on the other hand, ends much differently. Instead of baskets filled with miracle bread, there is a single plate with a severed head sliding around in its own blood. The guests may leave the banquet filled up, but also with a chilling reminder of how cruel and fickle their host is. They don't leave singing his praises but nervously wondering who might be the next victim of his—or his wife's.

Two Hosts

Then there is the contrast between the two hosts. Throughout his story of Herod, Mark takes great pains to show us how weak and insecure the man is. John the Baptist intrigues Herod, but John cannot bring the man to true repentance. In the face of Herodias' hatred of John, Herod devises a plan to protect the prophet that is riddled with flaws. He thinks that by keeping John in prison, he is showing his wife that he is strong and decisive. He thinks also that he is keeping John safe. But in reality, he is only bringing John within Herodias' grasp. All she needs is the right excuse, and John, unable to escape, can be dispatched.

Herod is also at the mercy of his guests. First, he over-promises (the bane of many a political leader), and then he finds that he has trapped himself in those promises. He cannot take back his words, for fear that his guests will spot a weakness they can exploit. He tries to look strong and in charge of events, but everyone there knows that events, and his wife's cleverness, have overtaken him. The only avenue open to him is the one he most wanted to avoid. So he orders the execution and hands the Baptist's head, on a platter, to the young girl.

Jesus, on the other hand, is completely in charge of the situation. Seeing how eager the crowd is to spend time with him, he scuttles his plan to get away with his disciples for some rest. It may appear that he simply gives in to the crowd's expectations just as Herod has done, but there's an important difference. Mark has already established that the crowds that Jesus attracted came mostly because they were looking for what Jesus could do for them: heal them, drive out demons, and the like. But as has happened before, Jesus doesn't perform miracles. At least not yet. Instead of doing all those works of wonder, "he began to teach them many things" (Mark 6:34). He meets the crowd on his own terms and according to his own agenda. They may have been wanting to see more miracles, but Jesus knows what they really need: his word.

Of course Jesus wasn't being stingy. He was motivated, above all else, by compassion for them. But it's not the false compassion of the overly indulgent. Herod might congratulate himself for feeding his subjects so lavishly, but he doesn't give them what they need. And what he does give, he gives only to those who are already well off.

Jesus, on the other hand, acts like a true shepherd. He knows what his sheep need, and he goes out of his way to give it to them. Mind you, Jesus doesn't begrudge the crowd a miracle or two. When the right time comes, he performs one of his greatest miracles: he takes five loaves of bread and two fish and multiplies them so that he can feed thousands. But again, it's a work of compassion. The people's need for food was real, and he met their need willingly, happily, and completely.

A Compassionate Shepherd

It's a common assumption that Mark paints Jesus in a harsher light than the other Evangelists. And that's true, but only to a certain extent. Yes, Jesus is more direct in rebuking and correcting his disciples. Yes, he appears dismissive toward his mother and brothers and sisters. Yes, his parables have a sharper edge. But Mark doesn't give us only the tough-love version of Jesus. He also shows how tenderhearted Jesus is, and this story is one of the clearest examples of how much he loved the people around him and wanted nothing but the best for them.

For Reflection

1. Imagine that you are one of the guests at Herod's banquet. Perhaps you are, like Matthew, a supervisor of tax collectors. Maybe you are the wife of one of Herod's governors. What do you think the conversation at your table would sound like? How do you and your fellow dinner guests react when Herod presents Herodias' daughter with the severed head of the prophet John?

2. Now imagine yourself as part of the crowd that caught up with Jesus and derailed his plans for some rest. Perhaps you are a fisherman, like Peter and Andrew. Maybe you are a widow with three small children. You have come to see what new wonders Jesus will perform, but instead he begins teaching. What do you hear him saying? What kind of effect do his words have on you?

3. Many scholars and saints see in this story of the multiplication of the loaves a foreshadowing of the Last Supper and, even more so, of the gift of the Eucharist that we celebrate every Sunday. Apart from the obvious theme of bread that Jesus blesses, breaks, and shares, what other parts of this story remind you of the Mass?

How are you like—and how are you unlike—the people Jesus fed that day?

4. Think of all we have said about the crowd in Mark's Gospel. Jesus knows by now how fickle the people are, even how dangerous they can be. Still, he feels for them and teaches and feeds them. What do you think is going through his mind in this story when he suspects that he will have to change his plans to care for them? What do you think goes through his mind when he sees you coming through the doors of your church and settling in your pew? Imagine yourself there right now; what would you say to Jesus?

Ironies and Hypocrisies

Mark 7:1-30

"There is nothing outside a person that by going in can defile." (Mark 7:15)

D o you want to know one of the most common mistakes we make when we read the Bible? We fragment it. We take the chapter and verse divisions too seriously. The same goes for the subheads that appear in most of our translations.

Mark never wrote in chapters and verses, and he didn't use subheads. Neither did Matthew, Isaiah, Paul, or John— or anyone else, for that matter. The chapter divisions we use today were developed in the year 1227, and the verses were added three hundred years later. The Geneva Bible of 1560 was the first English translation to use chapters and verses. Up till that point, the only delineations that appeared in manuscripts of the Bible were the title of each book and the number of each psalm.

Of course, these units of division serve a useful purpose: they help us break the text into manageable sections. But if we rely on them too much, they can lead to a kind of fragmentation of the word of God that the original authors never intended. Connections between "chapters" are lost; overarching themes are obscured. And if we take it too far, we pull verses out of context and say they mean something the author—and the Holy Spirit—never intended.

Just Another Skirmish?

Take today's passage, for example. It begins with some scribes and Pharisees noticing that Jesus' disciples were eating without first washing their hands. These observers weren't concerned with the transmission of disease, as we might be. They were concerned that the disciples were risking spiritual contamination. A Gentile may have handled their food, rendering it impure. Or the disciples may have come into contact with a Gentile and become impure themselves.

So the more fastidious Jews purified everything. And if they didn't, it meant their faith was defective. Or worse, *they* were defective. So these scribes and Pharisees, who seem to have been among the most fastidious, were calling into question the disciples' commitment to their faith.

All that is easy to understand, but here is where the fragmentation comes in. If we were to read this story on its own, we might see it as just another skirmish Jesus had with his opponents. Or we might take it only as a moral tale about paying attention to the defiling elements that arise within our own sinful heart. But if we read it in light of what has come before, we see that Mark is after something that is just as important, if not more so. Let's backtrack a bit so we can take a broader look.

Uncovering the Irony

Three scenes before this one, we read about Jesus multiplying loaves and fishes. In that story, Mark tells us that the disciples gathered twelve baskets of leftovers (see 6:43). Then immediately after that, Jesus walks on water and saves the disciples from a storm at sea (see 6:45-52). Then they came ashore and encountered a crowd of people begging for healing. From there, they traveled on foot back to their home in Capernaum, where this scene takes place.

If we read all these stories together, we'll see just how ironic the present story is. We'll also see how hypocritical the Pharisees and scribes were.

Let's start with the irony: even though there is an artificial chapter division here, Mark is still telling stories focused on the theme of bread. First, there's the multiplication of the loaves. Then, in the story of Jesus walking on the water, Mark inserts a comment to make sure we don't lose sight of the bread: "They did not understand about the loaves"

(6:52). Then comes a brief description of Jesus' power to attract people, followed immediately by the present controversial story—again over bread. Is it possible that when he introduces the Pharisees and scribes in the next scene, he wants us to imagine the disciples eating some of the leftover bread and fish that Jesus had multiplied a few days earlier? If so, this would be food that had come from the hand of God. Miracle food, in other words. But the religious leaders were upset about "human tradition" (7:8). Like the crowd that kept bumping into Jesus but not experiencing his healing power, these men were in the presence of the miraculous, but they couldn't see it.

Exposing the Hypocrisy

As for the hypocrisy, the Pharisees and scribes in this story were insinuating that the disciples had placed themselves *outside* of God's favor by eating in an unclean state. But everything we've seen the disciples do—from preaching and healing people on their missionary journey to assisting in Jesus' miracle of the loaves to witnessing him calming the storm—shows that they are about as close to being *inside* as possible.

Despite that, these religious leaders kept asserting their own insider status as the truly observant, but everything they said and did showed how far outside they really were:

- Instead of giving of themselves to care for the needy, they spent their time finding fault with the very people who were doing this important work.
- Instead of sharing bread with hungry strangers, they imposed tighter and tighter restrictions on what foods people could eat and with whom they could eat.
- Instead of joining in Jesus' grand project of bringing people closer to God, they devised rules and regulations that drove people further away.
- Instead of going out to the margins to bring people in, they went right to the center—Jesus' inner circle—and sought to send them to the margins.

"The Things That Come Out"

With this story, Mark continues to show us who the true shepherd of Israel is. It's not Herod, the weak and easily manipulated ruler, and it's not the scribes and Pharisees with their concerns for human tradition and their blindness to Jesus' goodness. Jesus is the true shepherd. His compassion knows no bounds, and his commitment to his people is unwavering.

But Mark isn't just hashing over old ground here. Digging deeper into his contrast between Jesus and Israel's earthly leaders, he uncovers another layer of the sin and duplicity that motivated them: "the things that come out" of "the human heart" (Mark 7:15, 21). And by putting his finger on the interior drives that we all have in common, he shows us that everyone is answerable.

For Reflection

1. Try an experiment: read all of chapters 6 and 7 of Mark straight through a few times. Try your best to ignore the subheads and all other divisions in the text. Let the sweep of Mark's big-picture story sink in a bit. What new insights can you find?

2. Notice that the disciples seem to be more on the inside of Jesus' teaching and his intentions when they are going out to the margins as opposed to when they are alone with Jesus. It's when they go out to preach that they are able to do the things that he did. It's when they help feed the five thousand that they are acting like true shepherds. But it's when they're alone in the house with him that they fail to understand the parable about food. What do you think it is about going out to the margins that brings them closer to Jesus? Have you experienced something like this in your life?

3. Imagine you are one of the disciples, eating some of the leftover bread and fish, when the scribes and Pharisees voice their objections. Set the scene in your mind and let it play out. How do their words sound to you? How do they make you feel? What about Jesus' response to them? How does that make you feel?

4. Can you think of one way that we may be tempted today to "abandon the commandment of God and hold to human tradition" (Mark 7:8)? It doesn't have to be anything really big or scandalous. Is there some way that you have justified putting a teaching of Jesus aside in favor of something more socially acceptable? What do you think Jesus would say about this? How can you bring this action back into line with Jesus' words and his true intentions?

5. Look at the story of the Syrophoenician woman's faith at the end of today's reading (see 7:24-30). Jesus appears to refuse healing a woman's daughter simply because she is a Gentile, or a "dog" in common Jewish parlance. But when the woman persists, he heals her daughter. This story comes right after Jesus dismantles the distinction between clean and unclean foods. Having just done that, does it make sense for him to uphold a distinction between clean and unclean people? What do you think Jesus was doing here?

Still Deaf and Blind

Mark 7:31–8:26

"Do you have eyes, and fail to see? Do you have ears, and fail to hear?" (Mark 8:18)

Jesus does a lot of odd things in today's passage, doesn't he? First, he places his fingers in a man's ears, touches the fellow's tongue, and then . . . he spits and emits an audible sigh.

Later, confronted by some Pharisees demanding another sign, he sighs again, vows that no more signs will be given, and abruptly walks away.

Finally, he heals a blind man . . . again, by means of spit.

What do you think? Is Jesus having a bit of fun here? Maybe he's blowing off some steam or helping everyone to relax.

Or maybe Mark is deliberately using these details to move his story along. Yes, that has to be the real answer. He isn't just telling us about healings anymore. He's after something deeper. Something more important.

Why Is It So Hard?

The first thing to notice is that Jesus appears to struggle in healing both the deaf man at the beginning of this section and the blind man at the end. For the deaf man, Jesus groans, gives a sharp command, and appears to resort to special gestures in order to effect the healing. And for the blind man, Jesus' first attempt doesn't seem to fully take. The man can see, but everything is blurry and out of proportion. So Jesus has to give him a second dose.

Given everything we've seen so far, this doesn't add up. Jesus has already calmed a storm at sea without uttering a single word (see Mark 6:51). He has multiplied a few loaves and fishes just by saying grace (see 6:41). And he routed a whole legion of demons with a single command (see 5:13). Jesus has already done many more powerful things with seemingly little effort. So why struggle now?

New Territory

Because Mark is beginning to take us, his readers, into new territory. He uses these stories to tell us that we're entering a precarious phase in his story—what some might call an inflection point. Mark is beginning to pivot away from his focus on Jesus' dealings with the crowds and his detractors so that he can focus on Jesus' dealings with his disciples, especially those closest to him.

You'll see, as the next chapters advance, that things are about to get more personal, both for the disciples and for Mark's readers. No longer can they—or we—take solace in thinking we're better than the Pharisees and scribes who hounded Jesus. No longer can they—or we—consider ourselves superior to the fickle crowd always demanding more from Jesus. In fact, both of these parties virtually disappear from the scene. Between now and his entry into Jerusalem in chapter 11, Jesus interacts with a sizable crowd only once and with some Pharisees only once. For the rest of the time, he is either teaching his disciples privately or healing just one person.

We begin to see this new focus in Jesus' conversation with his disciples while they are in the boat after he miraculously feeds four thousand. When they fail to pick up on the warning embedded in an analogy he gives them, Jesus replies with his harshest words for them yet: "Are your hearts hardened? Do you have eyes, and fail to see? Do you have ears, and fail to hear?" (8:17-18).

Blind eyes and deaf ears. This should spark our memory in two ways.

Between the Brackets

First, Jesus has just healed a deaf man (see Mark 7:31-37) and he is about to heal a blind man (see 8:22-26). The two healings that appear to cause Jesus the most trouble form brackets around the stories between them. Included inside these brackets is the story of a second miracle of loaves and fishes (see 8:1-10). It's a familiar scene, and we should be surprised that the disciples seem to have forgotten about Jesus' ability to feed so many with few provisions. But here they are again, protesting that the need before them is too great. Blind and deaf indeed!

Included also is the demand from a group of Pharisees for a sign (see 8:11-13). Jesus, exasperated, refuses to comply with their request. Immediately afterward, he warns the disciples—who must have seen this exchange—against the "yeast" of needing an ever-increasing number of signs to validate Jesus' words (8:15).

You would think that having once seen Jesus feed the crowd, they would have the faith to believe that Jesus could perform the same miracle again. But no, they are too blind and deaf to perceive Jesus' power—and his compassion for the hungry. It seems they are no better off than Jesus' opponents, who are also blind and deaf.

Right in Front of Your Eyes!

The second spark to our memory takes us further back, to the parables in chapter 4. Having just heard the parable of the sower and the seeds, the disciples ask Jesus in private what it means. He replies,

> "To you has been given the secret of the kingdom of God, but for those outside, everything comes in parables; in order that
> 'they may indeed look, but not perceive,
>   and may indeed listen, but not understand;
> so that they may not turn again and be forgiven.'" (Mark 4:11-12)

Jesus is referring to the crowd—people who are also blind and deaf. These are the hangers-on. The ones satisfied with physical healings and material bread. The ones who will cheer Jesus as he "who comes in the name of the Lord" on Palm Sunday but who, mere days later, will cry out, "Crucify him!" (11:9; 15:13). The disciples are no better off than these people—and after all the time Jesus has already put into them! After all the explanations and guidance. After they themselves have healed the sick and cast out demons. Somehow, the disciples still don't get it, and Jesus upbraids them for it.

Blind eyes. Deaf ears. Hardened hearts. These are the future leaders of the Church. Clearly Jesus has his work cut out for him. And for the next three chapters, he sets himself to the task of opening their eyes, unstopping their ears and, most important, softening their hearts.

Am I Blind?

Reading these stories in Mark and following any good commentary or set of footnotes, you would know by now that Mark is placing his readers—including you—in the position of the disciples. You would get the hint that he is telling you about your own blindness and deafness. This is the point at which many readers might feel compelled to stop and examine themselves: "What am I not seeing about Jesus? How am I not hearing his voice?"

It may sound counterintuitive, but I'm going to ask you to avoid doing that. For two reasons. First, it's illogical. How can a person who is blind identify those things he can't see? How can someone who is deaf have any idea what another person's voice sounds like? The last thing you need to do is go rooting around in your heart trying to find the things you can't even see or hear. You may indeed come up with a list, but chances are you'll be wrong. Why? Because you're blind and deaf! It's like trying to fix your broken right arm with your right hand.

Second, you're only halfway through this Gospel. Mark still has a lot to say. So don't jump the gun. Give him a chance to tell his whole story, and then go back and ask those questions. Let Mark open your eyes—or better yet, let the Holy Spirit open your eyes—instead of trying to do it yourself. You'll likely find it a lot less confusing, a lot less painful, and a lot more hopeful.

For Reflection

1. Now is a good time to do a bit of review. Jesus has identified his closest disciples as people who are blind, deaf, and hard of heart. Surely this is no revelation for him! And surely Mark has been hinting at this throughout his story. So flip through the pages of Mark 1–7, and look at how Mark portrays the disciples. Look for the clues—some are subtle, but many are obvious—that these followers of Jesus have a long way to go before they can take on the responsibility of leading the Church.

2. By recounting stories of difficult healings, Mark is preparing us for his account of the disciples' spiritual blindness and deafness. In a sense, he's saying, "Healing physical blindness is a lot easier than spiritual blindness." Why do you think that is? What is so much more challenging about spiritual healing when compared to physical healing?

3. Go back to the beginning of Mark, when Jesus appeared on the scene calling people to repent and believe the good news. Recall how we said that this was primarily a call to a change of heart and mind. How might this call be related to the disciples' spiritual blindness and deafness? How might it be related to your own spiritual blindness and deafness?

The Messiah Revealed, Part 1

Mark 8:27-38

"You are the Messiah." (Mark 8:29)

This is one of those blink-and-you'll-miss-it moments. Jesus asks the disciples who they think he is, and Peter gives a four-word answer: "You are the Messiah" (Mark 8:29). We're a lot more familiar with Matthew's account, in which the story is much more dramatic. In Matthew, Peter proclaims Jesus not only as Messiah but also as Son of God. And Jesus, impressed with Peter's insight, blesses him and gives him a new name and a new role: the "Rock" of the Church (Matthew 16:18; see 16:13-19). Matthew deploys so much fanfare that it's clear Peter is saying something of great import and consequence—and that Peter himself is a person of great import and consequence.

The First Rebuke

Mark, on the other hand, treats the moment almost as if Peter should not have said anything. In fact, Jesus responds with a rebuke rather than a blessing: "He *sternly ordered them* not to tell anyone about him" (Mark 8:30, emphasis added). For Mark, this is not the glorious moment when Peter becomes the first pope. It's the moment that triggers the inflection point we talked about yesterday. And that inflection point comes, not in Peter's proclamation, but in what Jesus says afterward:

> The Son of Man must undergo great suffering, and be rejected by the elders, the chief priests, and the scribes, and be killed, and after three days rise again. (8:31)

This is the fulcrum on which Mark's entire Gospel pivots. From the very first verse, when Mark told us that he was going to write about "Jesus Christ [Greek for Messiah], the Son of God," he has brought us in on the secret of Jesus' identity and allowed us to watch as even his closest disciples struggle with understanding him. But now comes the moment when Jesus begins to tell *them* exactly what kind of Messiah he is:

- He's the kind of Messiah who lays down his life.
- He's the kind of Messiah who goes willingly to the cross as a sacrifice on behalf of the people he has come to save.
- He's the kind of Messiah whose self-sacrifice is so pure that it breaks the power of death itself.

The Scandal of a Rejected Messiah

Of course, none of this occurs to the disciples. And how could it? The mere suggestion that Israel's Messiah would meet with rejection and death was so foreign to them that they could not wrap their brains around it. And so, after Jesus rebukes Peter for proclaiming him Messiah, Peter turns around and rebukes Jesus for describing a disturbingly different Messiah than he expected.

Before we judge Peter too harshly, let's step back and look at some context. It's commonly assumed that Israel in the first century A.D. was a hotbed of messianic fervor. It's true that false messiahs and political activists posing as prophets sprang up on occasion, but most of that happened in and around Jerusalem. Reports of these uprisings in the holy city would occasionally make their way north to Galilee and ignite the imaginations of the more rural tradesfolk there, but for the most part, the people of Galilee—including Peter—enjoyed a relatively peaceful coexistence with their culturally Jewish leader, Philip the Tetrarch.

But whatever messianic hopes were burbling under the surface, Peter and the others clearly had seen something special in Jesus. Why else would they be willing to follow him so faithfully? And more to the point of today's passage, why else would they stick with him despite their inability to understand who he was and what he was about?

Something about Jesus kept drawing them to him, and part of that something must have been the hope, however dim, that he might truly be the longed-for liberator of Israel. There must have been the hope that Jesus was going to assume the mantle of David, the "anointed one" (which is what "messiah" means) par excellence.

Given all this, one thing was for certain: messiahs weren't supposed to meet a violent end. At least not at the hands of Israel's religious leaders. They were supposed to enter Jerusalem to the sounds of popular acclaim. They were supposed to receive a hero's welcome from the elders, rout their pagan oppressors, and usher in an era of justice and peace.

So you can imagine the cognitive dissonance that Peter and the others felt when they heard Jesus say, "quite openly" in fact, that yes, he was going to Jerusalem—but to his death, not his enthronement (Mark 8:32). And so Peter rebuked Jesus for making such an unexpected and disturbing prediction.

Back-to-Back Rebukes

Clearly Peter thought this was serious business. The Greek word for "rebuke" in this passage is the same word that Mark used to describe the way Jesus deals with demons (see 1:25; 9:25) and with the violent forces of nature (see 4:39). It is a stern, disciplinary word conveying the sense of a superior correcting his inferior. And that's what makes Peter's rebuke so striking. He was so scandalized by Jesus' words that a simple, innocent request for clarification wasn't enough. Neither was it enough to say, "Surely you don't mean that?" Jesus had gone too far, and Peter took it upon himself to admonish him.

But Peter wasn't all that successful. Mark tells us that Jesus cut him short and rebuked him in turn. "Get behind me, Satan! For you are setting your mind not on divine things," he says, "but on human things" (8:33). At this moment, Peter was no different from the demons that had also proclaimed Jesus' exalted status (see 3:12). His words were no different than the violent winds that whipped up the Sea of Galilee. At this moment, Peter was an opponent to Jesus and his mission, and Jesus had to make it clear how far from the truth he was.

Scandalized Disciples

It seems that Jesus wasn't content just to correct Peter's view of what kind of Messiah he was. Immediately after rebuking Peter, he calls everyone to himself—including, of all people, the crowd—and spells out for them what it means to be his disciple:

> "If any want to become my followers, let them deny themselves and take up their cross and follow me. For those who want to save their life will lose it, and those who lose their life for my sake, and for the sake of the gospel, will save it." (Mark 8:34-35)

Quite apart from the idea that the Messiah would be rejected, Jesus saw another reason why his disciples were scandalized. If Jesus were going to lead a victorious rebellion and take up the throne of David, then there was a pretty good chance that his closest followers would receive roles of honor and glory alongside him. An acclaimed, triumphant Messiah would naturally have acclaimed, triumphant lieutenants. As for the lieutenants of a rejected, executed Messiah—well, it didn't take too much imagination to see that the gallows probably awaited them as well.

So it was vital that Jesus make it very clear not only what it meant for him to be the Messiah, but also what it meant for them to be his disciples. They had to be willing to lay down their lives, if necessary, for the sake of Jesus and his gospel.

Eyes Partially Opened

This is the inflection point for Peter and the disciples. It's also the inflection point for all of Mark's readers, including us. It's the moment when everything Jesus has said and done so far becomes intensely personal. For the next three chapters, Mark will take us on a journey to Jerusalem with Jesus and his disciples. On this journey, we'll see how the disciples are brought face-to-face with Jesus' messiahship of self-sacrifice and their call to a discipleship of similar self-giving.

At this point, the disciples' eyes have been opened to who Jesus is, but just as it was for the blind man from Bethsaida, their vision is only partial (see Mark 8:22-28). Tomorrow we'll see how Jesus offers them—and us—a clearer vision on the Mount of Transfiguration. And we'll begin to see how hard it is for them—and us—to accept that vision.

For Reflection

1. Take a closer look at Mark 8:32-33. Mark offers a couple of "stage directions" that highlight the dramatic tension between Jesus and Peter in this pivotal scene. First, he says that before rebuking Jesus, Peter "took him aside." Then he says that before rebuking Peter, Jesus turned and looked at the rest of his disciples. Try to picture these movements. What was Peter's expression when he took Jesus aside? How did Peter redirect Jesus? Was he timid or gruff? Did he do it carefully and deliberately, or did he gasp, grab Jesus by the arm, and wheel him around? What was his tone of voice? Next, picture Jesus turning back to look at the other disciples. Did he shake himself free from Peter's grasp? Did he raise his hands, palms outward, in an expression of rejection? How did he sound when he uttered his rebuke of Peter? Sit with this scene for a bit, and see what thoughts or prayers come to you. What do you want to say to Jesus?

2. Every age and every culture seem to have their own fair share of messiah figures. Can you name a couple of them in the world today? Don't think only of politicians. Think also about social media influencers, celebrities in general, and even religious figures. How are these "messiahs" like Jesus? More important, how are they different from him?

3. Take a few moments to ponder Jesus' words about discipleship in Mark 8:34-37. Can you think of a situation in the past when following Jesus was costly for you? Maybe it had to do with a relationship that threatened to draw you away from Jesus. Maybe it was when you faced a particularly strong temptation and had to deny yourself. Bring the situation to the forefront of your memory, and talk with Jesus about it. What do you want to say to him now that the situation is past? What do you think he wants to say to you about it?

The Messiah Revealed, Part 2

Mark 9:1-29

"Listen to him!" (Mark 9:7)

We have spent the past two days talking about the blindness of the disciples. If anything will open their eyes, it has to be something as bright and amazing as Jesus' transfiguration! So, did it work?

Seeing, but Not Hearing

Maybe and maybe not. Mark tells us that Jesus took Peter, James, and John up the mountain with him and that at the top, Jesus was "transfigured before them" (9:2). The heavenly glory was so brilliant that even his clothing became "dazzling white" (9:3). That's pretty bright! And to top it off, we learn that Jesus was talking with two of the greatest heroes of ancient Israel: Moses, the lawgiver, and Elijah, the prophet.

Heavenly glory, saints from the past, a bright and shining light. You would think that would be enough to open the disciples' eyes. You might even hope they would try to eavesdrop on the conversation, looking for some insight into this staggering revelation.

But none of this occurred to them. Instead, Peter suggested building monuments to commemorate the glorious occasion. On one level, this is understandable. Mark tells us the three disciples "were terrified" and that Peter "did not know what to say" (9:6). But I still wonder: Why did Peter say anything at all? Why interject himself? Couldn't he have stayed quiet? Wouldn't you expect that such an awesome, fearsome sight would silence him?

It seems that God the Father had a similar thought. Because when his voice boomed out of the cloud, he seemed to be speaking directly to Peter: "This is my Son, the Beloved; listen to him!" (9:7). Perhaps this mountaintop experience healed Peter's blindness a bit, but he still seemed rather hard of hearing.

Listening Is Believing

And hasn't that been the problem all along? Think back to the early days of the disciples' time with Jesus. He had spent the whole evening healing people—all of which Peter and the others most likely saw—and the next morning, they tell him, "Everyone is searching for you" (Mark 1:37). Presumably, "everyone" was looking for more miracles, and the disciples thought that might not be a bad idea. Keep the good times rolling!

But do you remember how Jesus replied? "Let us go on to the neighboring towns, so that I may proclaim the message there also; *for that is what I came out to do*" (1:38, emphasis added). He understood his mission was principally one of preaching, not healing, and he told his disciples as much. Think back also to the parable of the sower and the seed. The disciples didn't quite understand what Jesus was getting at, so he explained it to them. What does the seed in good soil represent? The ones who "*hear the word* and accept it" (4:20, emphasis added). That explanation was aimed directly at the disciples, the only ones who heard it.

So by the time we come to this point in the story, Peter and the others have seen a lot: healings, exorcisms, miraculous feedings, calmed storms, and joy-filled hearts. But they still haven't begun to listen to Jesus, at least not closely. And that lack of hearing hindered their vision.

They were like the man in the previous chapter who, at Jesus' first intervention, could see, but only indistinctly. As a result, Peter may have been ready to proclaim that Jesus is the Messiah, but his vision of what kind of Messiah remained cloudy and ill-defined. And until he listened, he wouldn't be able to see.

And so here Peter is on the mountain, beholding the Lord in all his heavenly glory, and he misses the point. He defaults to the external, the tents of remembrance. He misses the internal—Jesus' conversation with Moses and Elijah—and that conversation's meaning for Jesus' mission.

Clarifying the Mystery

This is a vital, but often overlooked, point behind the Transfiguration: you won't really get to know Jesus by relying only on heavenly apparitions or works of wonder. You must "listen to him" (9:7).

In their 1965 document *On Divine Revelation*, the Fathers of the Second Vatican Council made this very point. Revelation, they wrote,

> is realized by deeds and words having an inner unity: the deeds wrought by God in the history of salvation manifest and confirm the teaching and realities signified by the words, while *the words proclaim the deeds and clarify the mystery* contained in them.[3]

You need both the miraculous actions of God and the teachings that explain them.

Mark seems to be telling us the same thing: it is entirely possible to witness all kinds of spectacular miracles, and maybe even to receive them ourselves, and still fail to understand who Jesus is and what he has come to do for us.

So listen to Jesus. Let his words find a home in you. Ponder them. Savor them. Turn them over in your heart and in your mind. Ask him questions in your prayer, and listen for his answers. Use a prayer journal to help you keep track of your thoughts and any insights you think God is giving you in his word. From time to time, look back over what you have written. You'll probably be surprised at how much God has shown you—and at how your relationship with him has deepened because of it.

For Reflection

1. What do you think Jesus and Moses and Elijah were talking about on that mountaintop? Do you think there was a message there that could have helped open Peter's eyes? How do you think that message could have changed Peter's heart and made him more open to Jesus and his true mission?

2. When Jesus and Peter, James, and John reach the bottom of the mountain, they discover that the other disciples have been unable to deliver a young man from demonic possession (see Mark 9:14-28). How do you think this story reinforces the main points Mark was making in his telling of the Transfiguration?

3. Imagine that you are there with the three disciples witnessing Jesus' transfiguration. Picture yourself on the mountain, with Jesus, Moses, and Elijah standing before you in glory. Don't imagine yourself as another

first-century disciple, but as the person you are right here, right now. After a short time of talking among themselves, Jesus and his companions turn and look toward you. What do you want to say to them? What do you think they would say to you?

The Salt of Discipleship

Mark 9:30-50

"Have salt in yourselves, and be at peace with one another." (Mark 9:50)

We tend to skip over certain sayings in Scripture, either because we don't understand them or because we don't consider them all that important. Often enough, however, if we spend a little time with these verses, we'll find a treasure trove of spiritual insight and challenge.

Take the verse above, for instance: "Have salt in yourselves, and be at peace with one another" (Mark 9:50). It comes at the end of a chapter filled with dramatic revelation, stern rebukes, and challenging teachings. We might be so taken with the account of the Transfiguration and the growing tension between Jesus and his disciples that we feel we've already wrung all the meaning out of the chapter. Not to mention the odd-sounding command to "have salt" in ourselves. What does that even mean?

I'd like to suggest that this verse plays a key role in this part of Mark's story. So let's spend a little time with it.

A Widening Gap

Jesus and his disciples have begun their journey from Caesarea Philippi in the North to Jerusalem in the South. Along the way, he continues to tell the disciples about his coming death and resurrection. But they don't seem to be getting the message. Worse, they "were afraid to ask him" (Mark 9:32). It's possible they had an inkling of what he was talking about, but even that little bit was too intimidating; and so they avoided the subject. What do the disciples end up talking about? Which one of them is the greatest.

The gap between Jesus and the disciples is only growing wider. Jesus is talking about his own self-sacrifice, and the disciples are fighting over their own self-advancement. Jesus is trying to prepare them for the trauma of his apparent defeat, and they're caught up with which of them will triumph over the others.

When Jesus learns about their argument, he responds as you might expect: "Whoever wants to be first must be last of all and servant of all" (9:35). Clear enough, right? Right.

So are we ready to move on to other topics? Not quite yet. Because Jesus isn't done yet. He next places a little child in front of them, puts his arms around the little one, and says, "Whoever welcomes one such child in my name welcomes me, and whoever welcomes me welcomes not me but the one who sent me" (9:37).

The Greatness of Children

We need to be careful how we read this last saying. We can't isolate it from what has come before. If we do, we risk losing the central thread of this part of Mark's Gospel.

Remember, in Jesus' time children weren't looked upon as the innocent cherubs we think of today. They were as close to non-beings as you could get. Children had no legal rights in first-century Palestine, and they had no moral claim on anyone other than their parents.

So to embrace and care for a child who was not your own was to take a radical step. It was also to take upon yourself a menial, inconsequential task. And this is exactly what Jesus was telling the disciples to do—care for even a little insignificant child. Welcome him. Make her feel valued and wanted. Take this low position, even if it means giving up a high position, and you'll find me there. And finding me, you'll find my Father.

This is true greatness in the kingdom of God. Or, to put it in starker—and more familiar—terms, he's telling them to deny themselves, take up their cross, and follow him.

In and Out—Again

We could also see the disciples' argument about who was the greatest through the lens of another theme that we have been following: as a dispute about who is in and who is out. The moment you label one disciple as the greatest, you automatically label the other eleven as not so great. They fall outside the inner circle. And distinctions like that—distinctions that often occur when no real difference exists—risk sowing discord within the group. The temptation to envy rises. So do temptations to arrogance, elitism, self-condemnation, and bitterness. All attitudes that threaten the peace among the Twelve.

But the disciples don't seem to grasp what Jesus is saying because right after this, John recounts their attempt to stop a stranger from casting out demons in Jesus' name (see Mark 9:38). This stranger was an "outsider," and the Twelve tried to keep him outside. There's a layer of irony here as well. They were upset with this fellow for performing a deed that *the disciples themselves* had just proved incapable of performing (see 9:14-29). These ineffective disciples were telling this man to stop being so . . . effective. Simply because he was not part of their group.

You can imagine the animosity this must have caused—not necessarily between the disciples themselves, but between the disciples and this fellow, and eventually beyond. It's not hard to picture the man telling people about how elitist Jesus' disciples were. It's not hard either to imagine the murmuring and gossip that resulted from this.

Jesus, the Patient One

Again, the disciples are not being agents of peace, and again Jesus draws their attention to the child who we can only suppose is still standing in front of them: "If any of you put a stumbling block before one of these little ones who believe in me, it would be better for you if a great millstone were hung around your neck and you were thrown into the sea" (Mark 9:42). Strong but necessary words. If you are so concerned with who is in and who is out, it's going to affect your ability to minister to people. You're also going to alienate and embitter the outsiders—which is the exact opposite of what a disciple is supposed to do.

I can't emphasize enough how important this point is—or how deeply ironic it is. If anyone was going to be justified in driving away people who didn't fit in, it was Jesus. And if we were looking for the best candidates of who should be driven away, it would be harder to find a more qualified group than the disciples. Again and again, they misunderstand Jesus. Again and again, they misrepresent his message. Again and again, they cause him to sigh in exasperation.

But Jesus never excluded them. He never set himself above them or told them they were not worthy to be with him. He just kept teaching them. Bearing with them. Even giving them opportunities to share in his ministry. Even giving them glimpses into his glory. Unlike the disciples, who so easily got caught up in self-directed thoughts, Jesus continued to pour himself out as a sacrifice of love for them.

Salt, Fire, and Peace

So what about that statement about salt and peace that didn't seem to make sense at first? To answer that, we have to look at Jesus' final words in this passage (see Mark 9:49-50)—words all about salt. Let's take them one sentence at a time.

Everyone will be salted with fire. It sounds odd to our ears, but it would have made sense to the disciples—or any Jew at the time. That's because salt was commonly used as a purifying agent in sacrifices offered at the Temple (see Leviticus 2:13; Ezekiel 43:24). And these sacrifices were typically burned on the altar.

So to be "salted with fire" is to be offered to the Lord as a sacrifice. Just as Jesus was going to offer himself as a sacrifice on the cross. Or more to the point, just as he had been offering himself as a sacrifice to the disciples and the crowds who constantly pressed in on him. And to say that "everyone" will face the same fate is to point back, yet again, to the command to take up your cross and follow Jesus, to "lose your life" or offer yourself as a sacrifice to the Lord.

Salt is good; but if salt has lost its saltiness, how can you season it? Salt doesn't lose its flavor. It's the nature of salt to be salty. But if sacrifices are offered half-heartedly, it's as if the salt has lost its purifying properties. It has lost its effectiveness in making the sacrifice valuable.

So if the disciples have lost their saltiness, it's because they have been making half-hearted sacrifices of themselves. They may have given up their homes and jobs to travel with Jesus, but they are not giving up their inner lives. They are more eager to sacrifice one another as "not so great" than they are to sacrifice their own reputation or position within their little inner circle. And they are more eager to sacrifice the ministry of outsiders like the exorcist than they are to sacrifice their supposedly vaunted positions of honor as Jesus' specially chosen disciples.

Have salt in yourselves, and be at peace with one another. In addition to its use in sacrifices, salt was also commonly used when entering into covenants (see Numbers 18:19; 2 Chronicles 13:5). To "share salt" with another person is to share a meal with them—a sacred, legally binding meal that united them in a covenant relationship. To share salt is to agree to live in peace with one another.

This is where everything comes together. By telling the disciples to have salt *in themselves,* Jesus is telling them that it's in their willingness to sacrifice themselves for one another that they will find peace with one another. There is a call to humility here, a call to put the needs of others ahead of their own needs. This is the way of peace, but the disciples have demonstrated, time and again, that they are not following that way.

For Reflection

1. Jesus waits until they reach his home in Capernaum before he asks them what they have been arguing about along the way. (Note that it's about a twenty-five-mile walk from Caesarea Philippi to Capernaum. That's a lot of time!) It's also in the home that he teaches them—again—about their call to follow him along the way of discipleship. Jesus often uses these quiet, intimate settings to help his disciples face their own slowness of mind and hardness of heart (see 4:10-11; 7:17-22; 8:14-21). What do you think is the benefit of this strategy? Has there been a time in your personal prayer when you have experienced Jesus, through his Spirit, helping you confront something uncomfortable inside your heart?

2. Jesus told his disciples, "If any of you put a stumbling block before one of these little ones who believe in me, it would be better for you if a great millstone were hung around your neck and you were thrown into the sea" (9:42). He says this in response to John's story about telling the "outside" exorcist to cease and desist. The Greek word for "stumbling block" here is *skandalise*, another form of the word *eskandalizonto* that we encountered in chapter 8 of this book. It's where we get the English word "scandal." Why do you think this exorcist might be scandalized by the disciples' words?

How do you think a "salted" life of self-giving sacrifice might be the antidote to acting scandalously?

3. Look back over the past week or so. Can you identify any time when you acted in a way that mirrored the disciples' resistance to the call to self-giving love? Take that event to Jesus in prayer. Review the circumstances—but don't try to justify yourself—and ask him how you can do better the next time.

Simplicity and Single-Mindedness

Mark 10:1-31

Jesus, looking at him, loved him. (Mark 10:21)

I hope you've been picking up on a particular aspect of Mark's portrayal of Jesus as we go along: Jesus is a demanding Messiah. Not unreasonably so. And not abusively so. But Jesus doesn't pull any punches. He knows that his call to discipleship is challenging. He knows how costly it is for people to put their faith in him. It involves a commitment to live a certain way, not just to accept some theological propositions. As we saw earlier, it's a call to *repent* and believe in the good news. To change our minds about what it means to live under the loving care of God.

Now that Jesus is getting closer to Jerusalem and his death on the cross, the all-encompassing nature of this call is becoming clearer. It's also becoming clearer that his enemies and the disciples misunderstand this call. Today's passage gives us three stories that highlight this contrast sharply.

A Permanent Union

First, we have a question posed by some Pharisees: "Is it lawful for a man to divorce his wife?" (Mark 10:2). Notice that they're asking a far different question than the one Jesus answers. They want to know how far a man can go if he is unsatisfied in his marriage. But Jesus doesn't tell them how far they can stretch the Law to suit their purposes. They are referring to the Mosaic Law, but Jesus takes them back further than that. In fact, he goes all the way back to the beginning, to God's founding purpose in marriage: "The two shall become one flesh" (10:8).

For Jesus, marriage is more than a social contract that can be dissolved by either party. It's the joining of two individuals in a bond so close that their very identities are changed. It's not a legal arrangement, but a mirror of divine love: "what God has joined together" (10:9). It's not that divorce isn't allowed; it's that it isn't possible. No human is capable of breaking such a divinely sealed bond. Even if the two enact a legal divorce, that divine seal remains.

Undoubtedly, this raises issues beyond our purposes here. We know that marriages break down. Divorce is commonplace, along with remarriage after divorce. Questions concerning spousal abuse, infidelity, and arranged marriages also arise. The Church addresses such issues in its teachings regarding the indissolubility of marriage, questions of sacramental validity, and the theology behind the granting of annulments.

Still, we have Jesus' words: marriage is meant to be permanent. And he makes sure that the Pharisees and his disciples are clear about this. Now hold this thought as we go on because we'll be coming back to it later.

Childlike Simplicity

Next comes the story of Jesus and the children. Mark tells us that Jesus "was indignant" when he saw the disciples trying to shoo them away (10:14). The Greek word here conveys more than annoyance or aggravation. It's a stronger word often used to describe someone who is both incensed at and hurt by an injustice. Jesus tells his disciples that the kingdom of God belongs to "such as these"—almost in contrast to the disciples, with their gatekeeping tendencies (10:14). He tells them that if they want to enter his kingdom, they should imitate these children, not exclude them.

Why did Jesus treat these children with so much affection? Because of their innocence and tendency to keep things simple. They don't complicate matters. They don't play the angles or look for ways to get around their parents' commands—a marked contrast to the way the Pharisees just tried to bend God's law to their will. Of course, that doesn't mean that children are well behaved all the time, but at least you know—and they know—when they've broken the rules. They do it wholeheartedly, just as they do everything else!

Of Wealth and Treasure

Finally, we have Jesus' encounter with a rich young man, followed by a conversation with his disciples. Again, we see Jesus challenging a man who is trying to get into the kingdom on the basis of the Law of Moses (see Mark 10:19-20). You can understand his perplexity when Jesus tells him that obeying the commandments isn't enough. Surely this was an impressive fellow, but all that goodness he was relying on still couldn't get him where he wanted to go. Not even the fact that he was wealthy—despite the popular belief that riches were a sign of God's blessing—helped him. No, he had to divest himself, to become poor as Jesus was.

Why was Jesus so insistent? Because he wants us to do more than adhere to a code of conduct. He wants our hearts to be undivided, similar to the way he expects husbands and wives to be undivided in their devotion to each other. This rich young man, by contrast, was divided. His heart was attached to his wealth more than to the Lord.

Jesus wants disciples who are humble and detached, not followers who are so enmeshed in the world that they can't give him their hearts. He also wants disciples who are willing to find themselves on the outside of "respectable" company because he knows that following him will ultimately take them to the margins, where they will minister to the poor.

The disciples' response to all of this is telling. They are considerably less wealthy than this fellow. Not only do they not have much money, but they have also left behind their homes and jobs to follow Jesus. If material poverty were the only criterion for entry into the kingdom, you'd be more likely to see them relieved, comfortable in the thought that they had a fighting chance.

But Jesus' response paints a bigger picture for them. Material poverty is not a magic key that guarantees entry into the kingdom of heaven. There are other kinds of riches, and they need to be set aside as well. There can be great wealth, for instance, in the influence you have over other people. Your level of education could be another source of riches, as can a talent or ability that you value highly. Anything that you treasure more than Jesus and his kingdom can become an obstacle.

Single Minds, Simple Hearts

If there's one idea that ties these three stories together, it's single-mindedness. Jesus wants husbands and wives to be single-minded in their commitment to each other. He praises and blesses the single-mindedness of the children—all they wanted was to be with him. And he challenges the rich young man, as well as his disciples, to be single-minded in the way they treasure him.

There is no room for a divided heart in the kingdom of God. Jesus doesn't want his disciples to surrender to the conflicts that naturally arise when they set out to follow him. That sounds extreme, and in some ways it is. But Jesus doesn't see the world in black-and-white, and he doesn't see us that way either. He doesn't reject people who are divided. He knows us too well.

He knows that we all experience a spiritual tug-of-war within ourselves. It may be a conflict between the false security of wealth and the true peace of a simple life. It may be as complex as a conflict between loving our spouse faithfully and looking for a sense of escape or adventure in someone else's arms. Or it may be as simple as a conflict between being faithful to our daily prayer and sleeping an extra half hour.

There are a million and one potential conflicts that can arise in our hearts. Many of them may even show up at the same time. But Jesus wants us to constantly strive for the simplicity of little children and the wisdom and patience evident in stable loving marriages.

He "Loved Him"

Jesus knows how hard this can be, and he makes that clear in his conversations with the rich young man and with Peter. We may miss it, but it's there.

First, notice how Mark tells us that Jesus looked at the man and "loved him" (10:21). That's an unusual thing for

Mark to say. He seems to prefer to keep Jesus' love under the surface as something implied and understood, not directly stated. But here, he comes out and announces it.

It doesn't end there either. Twice Mark tells us that Jesus "looked" at his disciples as he told them about the lure of riches. The first time, Mark tells us that Jesus "looked around" at them, as if to capture the attention of all of them (10:23). And then, when the disciples' perplexity gives way to an astonishment bordering on anguish, Mark tells us that Jesus "looked at them" again and assured them that "all things are possible" with God (10:27).

If Jesus looked at the rich young man with love, how much more did he love the disciples who had given up so much for him? Imagine the compassion, the tenderness, the patience, and the understanding that he felt. Jesus wasn't against these disciples. He wasn't trying to make it hard for them. He knew already how hard it was. He knew the conflicts inside each of them and how much they wanted to be single-minded for him. He also knew how sorely each would be tested in Jerusalem as he gave up his life for them.

So here, in the middle of their journey to the holy city, he offers them words of encouragement and hope—even as he continues to challenge them and urge them to dedicate their whole lives to him.

For Reflection

1. Can you point to a time when you felt Jesus encouraging and comforting you as you were facing a struggle in your faith life? Take some time to write this out—if you haven't already. That way, you can come back to it when you are in a similar conflict. Let the memory of that time strengthen you.

2. Why do you think the rich young man "went away grieving" at Jesus' words (Mark 10:22)? Was it because he didn't want to lose his possessions? Is it possible it was also because Jesus didn't seem to show much deference to him for all of his "goodness" and wealth?

3. There's a lot of talk in these stories about marriage and children—Jesus even called his disciples "children" (10:24). Imagine that you are writing a homily on the theme "The Family of Christ." What do you think you would say, based on these three stories?

What Do You Want?

Mark 10:32-52

"What do you want me to do for you?"
(Mark 10:51)

Remember the man who was cured of blindness in stages (see Mark 8:22-26)? Remember how his healing comes right before Peter's profession of faith (see 8:27-33)? Just as the blind man first saw only partially, so Peter saw Jesus only partially: as the Messiah, to be sure, but not as the self-giving, suffering servant that God had called him to be.

Now it's James and John's turn. These two brothers—who, with Peter, made up Jesus' inner circle—believe that Jesus will enter into glory as he predicted, but they still can't come to terms with how he'll get there. In their request to sit at Jesus' right and left, they show that they want to share in that glory, but they haven't yet grasped that it will happen only as they drink the cup of suffering that Jesus will drink. They haven't grasped that Jesus came not to be served but to serve, and that they must follow his example.

And what do we have right after this story? Another blind man. It seems that the disciples haven't changed. Let's explore this blindness in terms of the question that Jesus asks James and John—and that he asks blind Bartimaeus.

The Hardest Question

What do you want? (see Mark 10:36, 51). This has to be one of the hardest questions to answer. Not "What do you want for dinner?" or "What do you want to do this weekend?" Just plain "What do you want?" What are the desires of your heart? What kind of person do you want to be? What do you really want from other people?

This, I think, is one of the central questions in Mark's Gospel. By telling the stories of such memorable people as the hemorrhaging woman, the father of the demon-possessed boy, and the Syrophoenician woman, Mark prompts us to ask, "What am I really looking for? Am I willing to press through a crowd to get it? Is it worth confessing how weak my faith is? What would I do if I were rebuffed at my first attempt?"

By placing Jesus' disciples in these stories, Mark offers us contrasting pictures: the stubborn faith of the hemorrhaging woman contrasts with the spiritual obtuseness of the disciples. The humble cry of the father, "Help my unbelief!" contrasts with the disciples' inability to cast out a demon because of their lack of faith (9:24; see 9:19). And the persistence of the Syrophoenician woman contrasts with the disciples' readiness to give up on her.

And now, just as Mark is about to begin his account of Holy Week and Jesus' Passion, he asks this fundamental question one more time, only a lot more directly—and with a much sharper contrast.

Contrasting Visions

Let's begin by drawing the obvious contrast: James and John want positions of honor, while Bartimaeus wants to be healed. James and John want to be seen and recognized, while Bartimaeus wants to see the world around him. It's a clear contrast of pride and humility.

Another contrast? Bartimaeus understands his need for healing. He sees that his life should change, and so he cries out for *mercy*, not just for physical healing. James and John, by contrast, don't see the need to change, and so they ask for honor and glory. They feel they're just fine the way they are and now it's time for everyone else to praise their excellent qualities.

There's also a rich irony here. James and John, the ones who want to be seen, make their request in secret. They pull Jesus aside to make their request so that the others can remain blind to their ulterior motives. But Bartimaeus, the one who wants to see, makes his request in public. Loudly. Repeatedly. With no concern for how he is perceived.

Where James and John use shadowy means in their quest for human honor, Bartimaeus has no problem announcing his need in his quest for Jesus' healing and restoration. And once he receives healing, Bartimaeus follows Jesus "on the way," as a disciple (Mark 10:52). James and John, by contrast, are trying to pave their own path, a path of glory and honor that is the exact opposite of Jesus' way of humility and service.

One final contrast: in both stories, Jesus asks, "What do you want?" (10:51; see 10:36). But when James and John make their request, he replies, "You do not know what you are asking" (10:38). They seem blind to what they truly want. All they have is some blurry picture of being enthroned next to Jesus—with no idea of what they'll do once they are there or why they should even have those seats in the first place.

Bartimaeus knows exactly what he wants, and he says it clearly and forthrightly: "Let me see again" (10:51). Jesus recognizes the clarity of Bartimaeus' spiritual vision, and so he tells him, "Your faith has made you well" and heals him (10:52). Bartimaeus then makes it clear he knows what he'll do with his restored sight: follow Jesus on the way of discipleship.

A Prelude to the Passion

Mark didn't just happen to place these two stories right before Jesus' entry into Jerusalem. Surely a number of other things happened on the final leg of their journey, but he intentionally selected these to highlight his theme of spiritual blindness among the disciples. Mark began exploring this overtly with his story of the blind man Jesus healed in stages, but this theme runs throughout his Gospel. From the moment when the disciples urge Jesus to come back into town so he can keep healing people (see Mark 1:35-38) to their confusion about not having brought enough bread with them (see 8:14-21), Jesus has been correcting them, rebuking them, and redirecting them.

These are Jesus' closest followers. The Twelve. The ones on the inside. You'd expect them to understand by now. But they don't. In many respects, they are no different from the Pharisees and scribes who opposed Jesus. Neither are they all that different from the ever-present crowd with its demands for more healings, its fan-club-like devotion to Jesus, and its disregard for Jesus' teachings. The only ones who seem to understand are the outcast: the blind, the deaf, the lame, the children, the unclean, and the sinful.

This contrast leads us right into the story of Jesus' Passion. In the next few chapters, the blindness of the disciples, Jesus' opponents, and the crowd will become increasingly obvious—with deadly consequences. All the while, Jesus will join himself with the outcast, the wounded, the sinners, and the children. And it will be from there, from that place of the despised and rejected victim, that he will offer salvation to everyone.

For Reflection

1. Bartimaeus' cry to Jesus, "Son of David, have mercy on me!" (Mark 10:47), is the basis for the centuries-old Jesus Prayer: "Lord Jesus Christ, Son of the living God, have mercy on me, a sinner." What do you imagine Jesus was thinking when he first heard Bartimaeus cry out like this? Was he delighted? Intrigued? Disappointed? Annoyed? Why?

2. When was the last time you asked yourself, "What do I really want?" Today is a good day to revisit that question. Don't go looking for negative answers. Just sit quietly with that question in your prayer and ask the Holy Spirit to give you insight. Maybe write down a few thoughts as you pray and take them with you into your day. Try to pay attention to your thoughts and actions during the day to see if anything you wrote down rings true to your experience.

3. We all have spiritual blind spots—attitudes and assumptions that go against Jesus' call to follow him. As you look at your thoughts and actions today, see if you can identify one or two of these blind spots. Don't be discouraged by what you see. Instead, be encouraged—it's a sign that the Spirit is at work in you, seeking to bring you a little more into the light.

The Passion Begins

Mark 11:1-11

"Blessed is the coming kingdom of our ancestor David!" (Mark 11:10)

Do you want a clue that we are now entering new territory? Well, here it is. Up to this point, Jesus has repeatedly told people to keep his identity a secret. He even commanded the demons to keep quiet (see Mark 3:12). Not even his closest disciples were allowed to tell anyone about their vision of the Transfiguration (see 9:9). That was then. Now, however, Jesus has no problem openly announcing his role as the Messiah. In fact, he seems to be almost going out of his way to fulfill ancient prophecies about the coming of a new kingdom—and a new king.

Out in the Open

Consider the prophetic gestures involved in his entry into Jerusalem:

- First, Jesus knows exactly what will happen when he has two of his disciples go into the village and untie a colt for him to use—and everything happens exactly as he predicted.
- Next, the mere fact that Jesus has chosen to enter on "a colt that has never been ridden" is in itself significant (Mark 11:2). To ride on a "used" colt is to court uncleanliness, depending on who used it beforehand. (Remember the restrictions mentioned in 7:3-4 and our comments about the hemorrhaging woman in chapter 7 of this book.)
- There's also the prophecy from Zechariah 9:9, which speaks of Jerusalem's new ruler coming into the city "on a colt, the foal of a donkey."
- Add to that the fact that Jesus allows his disciples to pile their cloaks on the back of the colt, making a kind of throne for him.
- Jesus actually *rides* into the holy city. This too was unusual. It was customary for pilgrims to Jerusalem to make the final portion of their journey on foot, praying and singing as they went.

- Finally, there's the crowd, shouting praises to God and hailing Jesus as "the one who comes in the name of the Lord" (Mark 11:9).

Jesus seems to have engineered the whole event, down to the last detail. And when the crowd begins cheering and acclaiming him, he offers no objections. In fact, he appears to consent to the ruckus!

A Not Very Spectacular Spectacle?

Not only does Jesus depart from his previous strategy of secrecy, but he does it in a way that puts himself at risk. He knows how dangerous it could be, given the political climate of Jerusalem, to be riding a colt accompanied by cheering crowds. All the city needed—especially as it prepared for the Passover—was for another would-be messiah to roll in and stir up the rabble. Both the Jewish elders and the Roman occupying force would be very quick to try to suppress any hint of an insurrection.

Still, the fact that Jesus entered unhindered gives us a clue that his entry might not have been as grand as the epic movies of yesteryear portray. Mark gives us no indication that any Jewish or Roman officials took notice of the procession. And nowhere in his narrative does the word "crowd" appear. This could have been just a small group of admirers, maybe in the tens and not the thousands. The whole gathering could well have blended in with the larger crowd of worshippers coming for the festival.

This spectacle—however spectacular it was or wasn't—seems to have been for the benefit of Jesus' followers, not a provocation to the powers that be. And not only for his twelve disciples, but for whatever number of people constituted the "many" who hailed him (11:8). Jesus is telling them, this wide circle of followers and admirers, that yes, he truly is the promised Messiah. Yes, he had come to the center of Judaism to inaugurate the "kingdom of our ancestor David" (11:10). And they were there to witness it.

But as we'll see in the next couple of chapters of Mark, Jesus is setting up this spectacle in order to subvert it. Over the course of the next few days, he will once and for all show the crowd, as well as his disciples, what kind of Messiah he is—and it won't be the kind they are expecting. This will become even clearer in the next section, when Jesus curses a fig tree and then drives all the money changers out of the Temple.

An Anticlimactic Ending

But for now, Mark tells us that by the time Jesus comes into the Temple area after his clamorous entrance, "it was already late" (11:11). The crowds—however big or small—have dispersed, and the show is over. So Jesus enters the Temple area with only the Twelve and looks around, a solitary figure against the night sky. What does he see? What is he thinking? Mark doesn't say. Jesus simply takes in the scene. Perhaps he prays. Then he returns quietly to Bethany with his disciples.

For Reflection

1. What do you think? Was Jesus surrounded by a huge multitude when he entered Jerusalem? Or was his entry a much humbler affair? What evidence can you find in the text—or perhaps in the previous chapter—to back up your answer? Do you think it matters?

2. Imagine that one of the disciples asked Jesus what he was thinking as he scanned the vast Temple complex of outer and inner chambers, the massive colonnades, and the mysterious Holy of Holies. What do you think Jesus would have said? Was his voice filled with wonder and awe? Sadness? Anger? A mixture?

3. When you enter your parish church next Sunday, imagine you are entering for the first time. For years you've heard about this building and all that went on in it, but you've not yet seen it. What thoughts come to your mind?

A Barren Temple

Mark 11:12-26

"May no one ever eat fruit from you again."
(Mark 11:14)

Yesterday we saw Jesus close out his first day in Jerusalem by quietly looking around the Temple grounds. We wondered what he was thinking and what he was feeling. Well, today Mark gives us some answers. And they're more than a little ominous.

An Accursed Tree

Jesus' day begins on a much different note than his entry into the city the previous day. Then, the people acclaimed him joyfully as he rode into town enthroned on a colt, as the prophet Zechariah had foretold. But today he walks in, and instead of encountering excited worshippers, he encounters . . . a fruitless fig tree. And he curses it.

It's natural to wonder why Jesus was so cruel—especially since it wasn't even fig season. We'll get some answers in the next scene, but for now suffice it to say that the Old Testament prophets often used the image of a fig tree when they spoke about God's promise for a restored Jerusalem:

> I will remove the guilt of this land in a single day. On that day, says the LORD of hosts, you shall invite each other to come under your vine and fig tree. (Zechariah 3:9-10)

> Out of Zion shall go forth instruction,
>   and the word of the LORD from Jerusalem.
> He shall judge between many peoples,
>   and shall arbitrate between strong nations far away;
> they shall beat their swords into plowshares,
>   and their spears into pruning hooks;
> nation shall not lift up sword against nation,
>   neither shall they learn war anymore;
> but they shall all sit under their own vines and under their own fig trees,
>   and no one shall make them afraid. (Micah 4:2-4)

The time will come, the prophets said, when the Lord will visit his people and usher in an era of peace. At the same time, the image of the fig tree appears in oracles that describe God's disappointment in the people's failure to live according to his Law. Look, for example, at these verses from Jeremiah:

How can you say, "We are wise,
and the law of the LORD is with us,"
when, in fact, the false pen of the scribes
has made it into a lie?
The wise shall be put to shame,
they shall be dismayed and taken;
since they have rejected the word of the LORD,
what wisdom is in them? . . .
When I wanted to gather them, says the LORD,
there are no grapes on the vine,
nor figs on the fig tree;
even the leaves are withered,
and what I gave them has passed away from them. (Jeremiah 8:8-9, 13; see also Micah 7:1; Hosea 9:10, 16-17)

Jesus, the Lord, has come to Jerusalem. He has come to gather his people, to rescue them from sin and all its effects. He spent the evening surveying the Temple, perhaps to see if the people were upholding his Father's commandments or were ready to receive him. If they were, then the wonders of the new era would be manifest—even to the point of trees bearing fruit all year long. But all he found was a fruitless fig tree.

An Accursed Temple

When Jesus enters the Temple grounds this time, he is no longer the quiet observer from the previous night. Instead, he is the angry prophet denouncing the chief priests and everyone who works with them. And he does so not only in his words but also in his actions.

"Is it not written," he asks, "'My house shall be called a house of prayer for all the nations'? / But *you* have made it a den of robbers" (Mark 11:17, emphasis added). Of all the things Jesus could have accused them of, he zeroes in on "all the nations" and the Temple being turned into a lair for thieves. Some historical perspective might help us understand why.

It appears that Jesus was upset with the buying and the selling of sacrificial animals that the priests had permitted to take place in the court of the Gentiles. He is not protesting the sacrifices themselves, but that the animals were being sold in an area set aside for Gentile visitors to pray. It may have been a shrewd business plan to place the point of sale so close to the altar of sacrifice, but doing so made it virtually impossible for Gentiles to worship God.

For Jesus, this is the final straw. Jesus now knows that the Temple and the Jewish priesthood can no longer continue, as we'll see in a few days. The corruption runs too deep; the scandal is too widespread. All the opposition, all the faithlessness, all the pride and selfishness he has encountered in the North has come to a head here in Jerusalem. Now the only thing left to do is wait for the Temple's inevitable destruction.

It's also the final straw for Jesus' opponents. Mark tells us that immediately after this episode, the chief priests and scribes begin "looking for a way to kill him" (11:18).

An Accursed Mountain

Coming back into the city the next morning, the disciples notice that the fig tree Jesus had cursed is now withered. That's when Jesus tells them,

> "If you say to this mountain, 'Be taken up and thrown into the sea,' and if you do not doubt in your heart, but believe that what you say will come to pass, it will be done for you." (Mark 11:23)

If you say to *this* mountain. Notice the geography. Jesus and the disciples, who leave Jerusalem at night, head back the next day to the city that was built on Mount Zion. *This* is the mountain he is pointing to when he says these words. Just as Jesus brought about the withering of a tree, he will bring about the crumbling of "the mountain of the LORD's house" (Isaiah 2:2). What do we make of this?

I believe that Jesus is preparing his disciples for the time when the Temple will be no more and the faith of many will be tested. God may be preparing to abandon the Temple, but he will not abandon his people, and they shouldn't abandon him. "Have *faith in God*," he tells them (11:22, emphasis added). The Temple's destruction will undoubtedly be traumatic. Much will change, and they must be ready to move with those changes by holding fast to the Lord in faith.

For Reflection

1. Mark tells us that after Jesus cast out the money changers, "the whole crowd was spellbound by his teaching" (11:18). What was it about Jesus' teaching that caught their attention? Look at 11:17 for some clues.

2. Recall a time when you felt as if your entire life had been upended. It may have been because of a tragedy, but it may also have been because of a happy change in your life. Looking back with something closer to twenty-twenty hindsight, can you identify how God might have been using that situation to help deepen your faith?

3. Ever since he began his ministry, Jesus has made it a point to reach out to the "outsiders." He has touched people afflicted with leprosy. He has healed people possessed by demons. He has shown mercy to people whose illnesses have rendered them unclean. In this passage, we can see that the outsiders are the Gentiles who have been kept from praying in the Temple. We can also see the crowds he has taught in the Temple as outsiders. Has there been a time when you have felt like one of these outsiders? How did Jesus reach out to you and heal you?

By Whose Authority?

Mark 11:27–12:12

"It is amazing in our eyes." (Mark 12:11)

Here is another example of how the chapter and verse divisions added to the Scriptures could trip us up. We might read chapter 11 of Mark's Gospel as a self-contained account of Jesus' first two days in Jerusalem and then take up chapter 12 as simply a series of unrelated parables and of confrontations Jesus had with his detractors. But that's not how Mark told his story. This whole section—from 11:1 to 12:34—is actually a tightly knit and gripping account of Jesus' activity in Jerusalem leading up to his Passion. The only reason I've broken up the material is because there are so many riches in it, and I don't want to miss any of it.

A Confrontational Parable

At the end of chapter 11, we read about Jesus' encounter with "the chief priests, the scribes, and the elders" in the Temple (Mark 11:27). *Who gave you the authority to come into this holy place and cause such a disturbance?* they ask. Jesus' response—answering their question with a question of his own—might seem evasive to us, but he is actually following a long-standing rabbinic tradition. The purpose of Jesus' question was not to avoid answering but to try to reframe the question the religious leaders posed.

Jesus not only reframes their question but puts his questioners in a bind. Either they risk the crowd's anger, or they admit they do not take seriously the words of someone widely considered to be a prophet. At the same time, Jesus makes his answer clear: both he and John were acting under the authority of God. It was God who had sent John to prophesy against Herod and to challenge the religious elites in Jerusalem, and it was God who had sent Jesus to continue John's work by prophetically seizing control, so to speak, of the Temple.

Now here is where the chapter divisions might not work in our favor. Chapter 11 ends with Jesus saying, "Neither will I tell you by what authority I am doing these things" (11:33). Then chapter 12 begins with "Then he began to speak to them in parables" (12:1). But Jesus' parable about the wicked tenants is not a new thought or a new encounter or a new section. It is the *continuation* of Jesus' answer to the question "By what authority are you doing these things?" (11:28). And not just a continuation, but a dramatic illustration of his answer.

The question of authority is at the heart of Jesus' parable, just as it was the source of contention between him and the chief priests, the elders, and the scribes. The tenants of the vineyard refused to acknowledge the authority of the landowner who had sent the servants to them. Neither did they accept that same authority when the landowner's own son came to them. Jesus is the "beloved son" in the parable (12:6), and he is also the beloved Son who has cursed a fruitless fig tree and cast out money changers from the Temple. The scribes, chief priests, and elders are the tenants who now plot against him, withholding the fruit that is rightly his.

Against Them

Notice how the chief priests, the elders, and the scribes react to the parable: they realize that Jesus was speaking *against* them. Not about them, but against them. They understood that this parable was Jesus' answer to their question about Jesus' authority. Not only was Jesus divulging the One by whose authority he was operating, but he was also telling them that they had forfeited their own authority over the Temple. Jesus wasn't just answering them; he was denouncing them as well.

They also realize that they have been unmasked. Jesus' parable about a son falling victim to the vineyard's tenants reveals that he was fully aware of their plot to have him killed. How he knew that was beyond them, since they seem to have kept their plans close to the vest.

It Is . . . Amazing?

Finally, Jesus ends his parable with what appears to be a misplaced quotation from the Hebrew Bible:

> "Have you not read this scripture:
>   'The stone that the builders rejected
>   has become the cornerstone;
>   this was the Lord's doing,
>   and it is amazing in our eyes'?" (Mark 12:10-11)

Many scholars believe that his quotation from Psalm 118 was tacked on later as a kind of "proof text." They cite other passages where this quotation occurs, like Acts 4:11 and 1 Peter 2:7, as evidence that it was the first Christians who saw the connection between this psalm and Jesus. But I don't agree. I think this quotation comes from Jesus himself. I also believe that it is central to the story that Mark has been telling all along.

Jesus understood that he would be rejected by the "builders." In fact, throughout his ministry he has been the subject of rejection, suspicion, and calumny from Israel's leaders. From the moment he began to look toward his journey to

Jerusalem, he warned his disciples that this would happen. Now he is standing before the very people who have the power to hand him over for execution, and he tells them that he knows they are plotting his death.

Everything is happening as Jesus knew it would. He could have stopped it at any point. He could have retreated to Capernaum and lived as a quiet carpenter or rabbi in one of the local synagogues. But he didn't. He continued on his course. You might even say that by overturning the tables in the Temple, Jesus lit the fuse himself. And even as that fuse continues to burn, even as the chief priests and elders and scribes conspire against him, even as his own disciples persist in their blindness and deafness, Jesus proclaims that his rejection is God's own doing—and it is amazing. Wonderful. Awe inspiring. A very, very good thing.

Who is the one with all the authority? Jesus. And he is exercising it by laying it down—not by demanding that he be served, but by serving, by giving his life as "a ransom for many" (Mark 10:45).

For Reflection

1. By whose authority? Pick any story from Mark's Gospel, and read it a couple of times. How do you think it reveals Jesus' authority? Look a little closer now. How does it reveal Jesus exercising that authority as a servant and not as one lording it over other people?

2. Do you think that Jesus' servant-leader approach to authority has implications for other positions of authority? Think, for instance, of the pastor of a parish. Or parents' relationships with their children. Or employers and their employees.

3. What is your experience of authority—both as one having authority and one giving someone else a degree of authority over you? Would you say it is more oppressive or more liberating? Note, of course, that there may be different answers for different relationships and that there is no right or wrong answer to the question. That's okay. Just spend some time reflecting on your experience and asking God to give you insights into how your experience can more closely mirror Jesus' teaching.

Many Questions, One Clear Answer

Mark 12:13-44

"This poor widow . . ." (Mark 12:43)

Where's the fruit? That question seems to hang over Jesus during his time in Jerusalem. First, he encountered a barren fig tree. Then, he discovered how barren the Temple had become. He then told the chief priests, scribes, and elders a parable about a landowner seeking fruit from his tenants. They understood his point: *they* were the wicked tenants who refused to bear fruit for their master. Now, in his encounter with the Pharisees and Herodians, as well as his encounter with the Sadducees, the theme persists. In fact, it persists through the rest of this chapter.

The Tables Turned

First comes a group of Pharisees and Herodians with their trick question about Jesus' policy on taxation. Once more, Jesus turns the tables on his questioners. They ask if it is lawful to pay the census tax to Caesar, but Jesus sidesteps the trap and tells them to render to God and to Caesar that which belongs to each. Or to put it another way, he tells them to *bear fruit* for God. The implication, of course, is that they have not been especially fruitful. Like the chief priests, scribes, and elders, these religious and political leaders have kept for themselves the fruit that should rightly go to God. Or worse, they have given it to Caesar.

Next comes a group of Sadducees. They present a story about a much-married but childless widow. They ask, with more than a little sarcasm, whose wife she will be once everyone has been raised from the dead. Jesus answers them with a quote from Exodus 3:6. "I am the God of Abraham, the God of Isaac, and the God of Jacob," he says. "He is God not of the dead, but of the living" (Mark 12:26-27).

If we were looking for a fresh biblical defense of the doctrine of the resurrection, this passage might just fit the bill. But if we were to read this story in sequence with the stories that come before it, we would see that once more we are facing a story about fruitfulness. This time, the central image is a woman who, for whatever reason, is unable to bear the fruit of children. To use biblical language, she is about as "barren" as the Temple has become—about as barren as the Sadducees who are questioning Jesus.

"You Are Not Far"

This is quite a bleak portrayal of Israel's leaders. Pharisees, Sadducees, Herodians, scribes, chief priests, elders—so many of them are barren, incapable of rendering to God the fruit that he is looking for. Like the fig tree Jesus encountered on his way to the Temple, they too have failed at their mission. And for that, they are accursed.

But not all of them. For after Jesus' encounter with the Sadducees, one singular scribe approaches him. He has not been sent by the chief priests and scribes as the others have been. Neither is he playing gotcha with Jesus. His question is sincere; he is only seeking the truth, and that's exactly what Jesus gives him. The entire Law of Moses can be summed up in two simple commands: love God with everything you have, and love your neighbor as yourself (see 12:29-31). And Jesus' words find a home in this man's heart, as they did not for the other questioners.

At last! Jesus has found someone who is genuinely interested in bearing fruit for God. Here is one who is "not far from the kingdom of God" (12:34). He is like a glimmer of light in the midst of the gloom and darkness gathering around Jesus.

In this brief exchange, all the schemes of Jesus' opponents are unmasked. "After that no one dared to ask him any question" (12:34). Any further attempts to trip Jesus up would be futile, for they would be seen in the light of the two great commandments. It would be clear that those who questioned Jesus would not be motivated by love of God or love of neighbor. The hatred, the arrogance, the murderous intent—it would all be laid bare, and the interlocutors would be shown for who they truly are. So Jesus' enemies retreat back into the darkness and wait for other opportunities to ensnare him.

She Has Given More

After recounting Jesus' words of warning against the now-exposed hypocrisy of the chief priests and scribes (and, by extension, their co-conspirators), Mark ends Jesus' second day in the Temple with a poignant scene: a poor widow puts two small coins—"all she had to live on"—in the Temple treasury (12:44). Jesus sees her and points her out to his disciples. Her act of generosity is a living embodiment of Jesus' words to the one sincere scribe. More than anyone else that day, she has rendered unto God that which belongs to God: her whole self. By contributing her last coins to the Temple, she has shown a complete love for God and his people. She, more than anyone else, has borne fruit for God.

But as heroic as this woman's donation is, it occurs under a dark cloud. Just before this scene, Mark recounts Jesus' warning about the scribes who, among other things, "devour widows' houses" (12:40). I don't think it's an unfortunate coincidence that Mark has placed these two scenes side by side. I believe that he is pointing to the woman as a prime example of one of the widows who have been reduced to abject poverty while the scribes continue to enrich themselves and their Temple.

By pointing her out just before he recounts Jesus' prediction of the destruction of the Temple (see 13:1-2), Mark gives us a most moving illustration of why Jesus feels the way he does about the Temple. People like this woman are trying their best to bear fruit for God. They are giving as much as they can—in some cases more than they should. And yet their gifts are ending up in the wrong hands; they are being used for self-serving purposes, not for the glory of God or the benefit of his people.

For Reflection

1. It's pretty clear why the elders, the chief priests, and their surrogates tried to appear sincere and righteous when they were questioning Jesus: they didn't want the crowd to suspect that they were plotting his death. Do you think the people could see through their false front? Why or why not?

2. The scribe who asked Jesus about the greatest commandment understood that loving God and loving one another were "much more important" than offering sacrifices to

the Lord (Mark 12:33). Can you think of anything that would count as a modern-day equivalent to these kinds of offerings?

3. The two great commands to love God with all we are and to love our neighbor as ourselves are absolute. Either you are loving God with your whole heart, or your love is impure, mixed, and divided between God and the things of this world. The same could be said about loving one another. But on nearly every page of the Gospels, we see Jesus welcoming sinners, treating them with respect, compassion, and patience. What do you suppose Jesus thinks when he looks into your heart? In your prayer today, imagine Jesus sitting across from you. What do you think he most wants to tell you?

Creation Upended

Mark 13:1-37

"Not one stone will be left here upon another."
(Mark 13:2)

Did you know that some Jewish traditions considered the Holy of Holies in the Temple as the "navel of the world"? According to this tradition, the entire Temple complex rested on the Foundation Stone marking the center of the world, with the Holy of Holies at the center of the center. That place, where God sat "enthroned upon the cherubim," was the meeting place of heaven and earth (Psalm 99:1). That's why only the high priest was allowed to enter that sacred space and, even then, only after he had performed meticulous purification rites to cleanse himself from all sin.

You can appreciate, then, how chilling the disciples found Jesus' words when he told them that "not one stone will be left . . . upon another" in the Temple and that "all will be thrown down" (Mark 13:2). No wonder only his four closest disciples—Peter, James, John, and Andrew—had the courage to ask when this would happen. If the Temple were to crumble, then all of creation would be at risk.

Creation Dissolved

It seems their fears are justified. When the disciples nervously question Jesus, he launches into his longest discourse in the Gospel of Mark. And what an unsettling discourse it is! In the course of this monologue, he describes:

- the breakdown of truth itself, with his prediction that many "false messiahs" will arise (13:22; see 13:6, 21-22);
- the breakdown of civil order, evident not only in "wars and rumors of wars" but also in the disciples being falsely accused in kangaroo courts (13:7; see 13:8-11);
- the breakdown of family life, the very heart of society, as "children will rise against parents and have them put to death" (13:12);
- the breakdown of the created order itself, as "the sun will be darkened, / and the moon will not give its light" (13:24; see 13:25).

All of these calamities will happen because the Temple, and its entire apparatus of worship and sacrifice to the Lord, will be destroyed. And as we saw yesterday and the day before, the Temple is doomed to fail because the chief priests and their acolytes have rejected Jesus. Because of the corruption of Israel's leaders, creation itself will unspool at a swift and terrifying pace. Israel, which was meant to be a "light to the nations," has unleashed darkness and gloom instead (Isaiah 49:6). Jerusalem, the center of the universe, will crumble and take everything with it.

Beware!

This seems like an appropriate way for Mark to describe Jesus' time in Jerusalem, doesn't it? Beware! From the moment when Peter proclaimed him the Messiah and he began his journey to the holy city, Jesus has been predicting nothing but trouble. In some cases, he even seemed to be courting it.

But it's not all doom and gloom. Throughout his discourse, Jesus weaves words of encouragement and hope. He tells his disciples not to worry when they are arrested and brought before tribunals because the Holy Spirit will give them the words to say in their defense (see Mark 13:11). He tells them that "the one who endures to the end will be saved" (13:13). He even says that God has decided to shorten the duration of these crises "for the sake of the elect" (13:20). In other words, Jesus tells them that he has their backs, even in the midst of all these catastrophes. He'll take care of them and help them come through everything safe and sound.

Take a moment and ponder these words. These men have not been model disciples, have they? They constantly misunderstand Jesus. They're concerned for their own comfort instead of the needs of the people Jesus ministers to. They get caught up in arguments about which of them is the greatest. They even plot and scheme against one another.

Many are the times that Jesus has rebuked them or corrected them or thrown up his hands in frustration over them. And yet he remains committed to them. He still loves them. He still tells them things he would never tell the general population.

As in the moment when Jesus "looked at them" and reassured them that God would help them enter the kingdom, Jesus here gives his disciples a message of hope and encouragement (10:27). He has already told them all they need to know in order to survive the coming upheavals—in his parables, in his lessons about humility and surrender, in his predictions of his own death and resurrection. Now they just need to beware the potential pitfalls that come when fear overtakes faith (see 13:5, 9, 33). And they need to remain alert and keep watch so they aren't taken by surprise when things begin to fall apart (see 13:23, 33, 35, 37).

An End and a New Beginning

But Jesus does more than make vague promises of spiritual help and predictions of a foreshortened time of catastrophe. In fact, as his discourse winds down, he gives these disciples a glimpse of what is in store beyond the trials and tribulations sparked by the Temple's destruction. Drawing from the end-times visions in the Book of Daniel, he tells them that the chaos will come to an end and that, ultimately, they would see

> "'the Son of Man coming in clouds' with great power and glory. Then he will send out the angels, and gather his elect from the four winds, from the ends of the earth to the ends of heaven." (Mark 13:26-27; see Daniel 7:13)

The vision in Daniel promises a time of fulfillment and restoration. It promises a time when God will win victory over his enemies and when the Son of man will receive a "kingship . . . / that shall never be destroyed" (Daniel 7:14). Destruction is not the end of the story. Neither is the unfaithfulness and rejection of Israel's leaders. To be sure, "heaven and earth will pass away," but Jesus "will send out the angels, and gather his elect from the four winds" and bring them into his eternal home (Mark 13:31, 27).

For Reflection

1. For centuries, Jesus' words against the Temple and its chief priests, along with his predictions of the Temple's destruction, were interpreted as a sign that God had permanently rejected Israel because Israel had rejected his Son. Political and religious leaders have used this false interpretation as an excuse to persecute and marginalize the Jewish people. This anti-Semitism reached its

ugly zenith in the Nazi concentration camps of World War II. But the Temple is not the same as Israel, and the chief priests are not the whole people of God. Read Jeremiah 31:1-26 for an example in Israel's past when God promised destruction and salvation for his people. What verses in this prophecy can you see that point to God's everlasting love for his chosen people?

2. Did you catch the reappearance of the fig tree in this chapter? All the fig tree stories in Mark 11 and 13 happen when Jesus is with only some or all of the Twelve. The crowd doesn't factor in, and neither do Jesus' enemies. Why do you think Jesus brought this up again? In what way does this fig tree story differ from the other two? What message is Jesus giving his disciples? What message is he giving you?

3. Think about a time when you knew that the Holy Spirit had given you just the right words to say in a difficult situation (see Mark 13:11) What signs can you point to that helped you believe that the Spirit was guiding you? Are you facing a situation now in which you could use the Spirit's help? Spend some time talking with him today, ask him for his guidance, and write down any sense or direction you think he is giving you.

In Remembrance of Her

Mark 14:1-11

"What she has done will be told in remembrance of her." (Mark 14:9)

Mark could have begun his narrative of the Passion with any number of incidents from Jesus' last couple of days in Jerusalem, but he chose to focus on Jesus' anointing in Bethany. The way he tells the story, by sandwiching it in the middle of another story, only heightens the drama already present in this moving story.

Mark begins with a discussion among the chief priests and scribes about their desire to arrest Jesus. His words and actions in the Temple have not led them to repentance.

On the contrary, these leaders have only hardened in their opposition to him. The only thing keeping them from arresting him is their fear of the crowd of worshippers who have come to Jerusalem to celebrate Passover. The last thing they want is a riot on their hands (see 14:1-2).

But Mark interrupts their conversation with a story about an anonymous woman who anoints Jesus' head and whom Jesus defends against accusations of being wasteful (see 14:3-9). Only then does he bring us back to the chief priests and scribes—this time with an offer from Judas that presents them with a golden opportunity to do the very thing they were discussing before the interruption (see 14:10-11).

While this might seem, at first, like an uneven way to tell his story, Mark makes it anything but. As he has done so many times previously, he offers us a carefully constructed study in contrasts. Let's focus on the story of Jesus' anointing to see how Mark does this.

An Extravagant Gift

The woman's gift is already striking: "very costly ointment of nard" was a luxury item, as was the alabaster jar holding it (14:3). By placing the story of this valuable gift alongside the story of the chief priests and scribes' debate, Mark highlights the value of her gift all the more:

- Her *public* display of devotion stands in contrast to the chief priests and scribes' desire for secrecy—and Judas' own clandestine meeting with them.

- Her willingness to spend something so precious as a way of *honoring* Jesus stands in contrast to the chief priests and scribes' willingness to spend money on someone who will *betray* him.

- Jesus unmasks the onlookers' *seeming concern for the poor* by telling them they can do good to them whenever they want. Mark implies that they aren't all that generous and that their objections are more for show than from sincerity of heart. This hypocrisy is dramatized in Judas' willingness to *take money for himself* in exchange for information regarding Jesus.

- Jesus understands his anointing as a preparation for his burial. He knows he is going to his death, and he speaks of it *openly*. And by doing so, he makes the chief priests and scribes' desire for *secrecy* seem futile and absurd.

- Finally, by anointing Jesus' head, this woman publicly *confesses* him as the Christ, the anointed One. This stands in stark contrast to the chief priests and scribes' *refusal* to accept him.

The Lowly and the Scorned

Once again, Mark shows us a true hero of faith. And once again, that hero is one you would not have expected:

- She is similar to the poor widow who donated her last two coins to the Temple (see 12:41-44). Not only are both of them women, who inhabit a lower social rank than men, but they both show deep, generous devotion to

God. Both are also presented in contrast to the wealthy and comfortable.

- She is similar to the Syrophoenician woman whose daughter was plagued by a demon (see 7:24-30). Just as that woman was an outsider because she was a pagan, this woman is an outsider because she doesn't belong at the dinner. She enters unannounced and uninvited, and her presence and her actions scandalize everyone there—except, of course, Jesus.

- She is similar to blind Bartimaeus, who also inserted himself where he wasn't invited (see 10:46-52). Despite the disapproval of the crowd, he persisted in calling out to Jesus for healing, just as this woman boldly broke with convention and anointed Jesus. Furthermore, Bartimaeus confessed Jesus as "Son of David," a messianic title, just as the woman acknowledged Jesus as Messiah by anointing him (see 10:47).

- She is similar to the children whom the disciples tried to shoo away from Jesus. As he did with the disciples in that story, Jesus rebukes the "gatekeepers" at the dinner and welcomes, even praises, this woman for seeing something in Jesus that the others could not.

Her Story Will Be Told

So this woman, with her extravagant gift and her deep reverence, takes her place with the other lowly and scorned heroes in Mark's Gospel. She is a true disciple and a true believer.

Jesus is so impressed with her, in fact, that he promises that "wherever the good news is proclaimed in the whole world, what she has done will be told in remembrance of her" (14:9).

This is high praise indeed! But there's more to Jesus' statement than words of praise. In pointing to the woman's reverence for him, her courage in disrupting the social order, and her generosity in anointing him as a suffering Messiah, Jesus reveals the heart of the gospel message. And that message is simple. Jesus' death will reveal him as the Christ. As the Christ, he is worthy of our devotion. And his call to repent and believe in the good news is meant to shake up the status quo and usher in a new way of relating to one another.

In telling this woman's story as part of his Gospel, Mark brings Jesus' words full circle: "What she has done will be told in remembrance of her" throughout the world (14:9). From now until the end of time, she will continue to show forth the kind of humility, devotion, and boldness that Jesus looks for in all his followers. Including us.

For Reflection

1. We have now entered Mark's Passion narrative, and the timing couldn't be better. That's because beginning with today, there are nine days left in this at-home retreat. That means you can treat this time as a kind of novena dedicated to Jesus' death and resurrection. If you haven't already, now would be the perfect time to start keep-

ing a prayer journal. Every day, take a few minutes to write down anything you read—whether in the passage itself or in this book—that strikes you as important. You could look for small details that remind you of something we've already discussed. Or you could write down one thing you can do each day to respond to what you've read. You could even write your own prayer of thanksgiving, worship, repentance, or petition. Who knows? Maybe, after the nine days have passed, you'll want to keep journaling.

2. No matter how hard they try, scholars and commentators have yet to come up with a definitive reason why Judas betrayed Jesus to the authorities. Some say it was because he wanted the money. Others say he was a frustrated revolutionary who grew disenchanted with Jesus' message of peace. Still others believe he was just trying to get Jesus and the chief priests in a room together so they could iron out their differences. In the end, we may never know. But that doesn't have to keep you from pondering this question: why do you think Judas did it? Look back at some of the central themes Mark keeps sounding, and see if any of them are helpful.

3. In your prayer today, imagine that you are a close friend of the woman who has anointed Jesus. You see her coming out of the house where Jesus is, and you go up to greet her. You can tell by the look on her face that she is brimming with excitement and can't wait to share

what has just happened. What do you think she tells you, not just about what happened, but about how it made her feel? What feelings arise in you as you imagine this conversation?

The Last Supper

Mark 14:12-31

"The Son of Man goes as it is written of him."
(Mark 14:21)

If you were to read only Mark's account of the Last Supper—not Matthew, or Luke, or John's—it's likely that one thing will stand out to you. Or at least, it stands out for me. And that is how much Jesus seems to be in control of the entire situation.

A Gathering Gloom

Try to imagine how various people are feeling as Jesus and his disciples gather for the Passover meal.

The two disciples Jesus sends into the city to make the preparations encounter things just as he predicted—as he had predicted also their procuring a donkey for his entry into Jerusalem a few days prior (see 11:1-6). But there's a different tone here. The first time, the message was that "the Lord" needed the donkey, and jubilant supporters surrounded Jesus as he entered Jerusalem (11:3). But this time, the two disciples are to refer to him only as "The Teacher," and a joyful entourage will not accompany him (14:14). Today, Jesus will enter the city quietly, almost secretively. As these two prepare the meal, they likely sense that something important is about to happen. But what?

Judas has already made arrangements to hand Jesus over to the chief priests and the scribes. So he must be looking about furtively, wondering if any of the other apostles are on to his plot. Or perhaps he's already feeling some regret for what he has done, but he knows the hole he has dug is too deep and he can't climb out.

The group gathers under the shadow of Jesus' confrontations with the chief priests, the scribes, some Sadducees, and some Pharisees. It seems that everyone with any power is against him. Some have been muttering about having him arrested, even killed. There is his long and troubling discourse about the destruction of the Temple and the chaos and dangers awaiting them as creation starts to unspool.

Everything seems so ominous now. And yet in the middle of all of this gathering gloom, Jesus is giving directions, prophesying, and leading the Passover prayers. He remains calm and self-possessed as the intrigue swirls around him.

He knows Judas is about to betray him. He knows Peter will deny him. He knows that all the disciples will desert him. Ultimately, he knows that "the Son of Man goes as it is written of him" (14:21). But he is not perturbed. On the contrary, he tells them that he will overcome all the forces arrayed against him: "After I am raised up, I will go before you to Galilee" (14:28).

Jesus remains the calm center of a gathering storm.

"Take . . ."

It's here, in the center of the storm, that Jesus offers the clearest and most dramatic revelation of who he is and of what he has come to do:

> While they were eating, he took a loaf of bread, and after blessing it he broke it, gave it to them, and said, "Take; this is my body." Then he took a cup, and after giving thanks he gave it to them, and all of them drank from it. He said to them, "This is my blood of the covenant, which is poured out for many. Truly I tell you, I will never again drink of the fruit of the vine until that day when I drink it new in the kingdom of God." (14:22-25)

The text is short, curt, free of the drama and emotion that Mark typically uses in his stories. But that's not because he thinks it's unimportant; on the contrary, it's because he wants it to stand out for his readers in all its stark beauty. For here, before his closest followers, Jesus is acting out, almost liturgically, what he will be doing quite literally the next day.

Take; this is my body. "Here I am, giving everything I am to you. I am holding nothing back, not even my very flesh. This is how deeply I am committed to you. This is how far I am willing to go in order to save you. All this time you have spent with me, I have been showing you what a life given over to God in love looks like, and you have been so slow to understand. But now, even as one of you is about to betray me and another deny me and the rest abandon me, let me show you one more time that I will *never* abandon you. Let me show you that I am willing and ready to lay down my life for you so that when it happens tomorrow you will know that I am doing this willingly."

This is my blood of the covenant. "Yes, this is my own blood. Through Moses, my Father entered into an irrevocable covenant with you—and he did it through the blood of a sacrificed animal [see Exodus 24]. But tomorrow I will shed my own blood. And when I do, I will be entering into a new and everlasting covenant with you. I will be binding myself to you by tasting a death that no immortal being has ever before tasted. You worry that the chief priests and scribes are going to take my life? They cannot take something that I am not willingly giving over. This is my gift to you—the gift of my faithfulness to my promises even as you continue to struggle to remain faithful to me."

A Gift Freely Given

All of this is contained in Jesus' few words and simple gestures. He knows that he is going "as it is written of him," and he wants his disciples to know that he is going willingly, of his own accord (14:21). He wants them to know that even when he is fastened to the cross, he will still be completely free. He will still be the Messiah, the Son of God who freely laid down his life for them. Even when his enemies believe they have triumphed by taking his life, he wants them to see in his death a perpetual gift of his life—his own body and blood.

For Reflection

1. What do you think was going through Jesus' mind as he looked around the table at the Last Supper and realized that all of his closest friends would abandon him, leaving him to face his death alone? How do you suppose he felt? How did this knowledge affect his thinking as he offered them the bread and wine?

2. Mark doesn't include Jesus' command "Do this in remembrance of me" (1 Corinthians 11:24). But he does use something like these words in response to the woman's act of anointing him with costly perfume: "Wherever the good news is proclaimed in the whole world, what she

has done will be told *in remembrance of her*" (Mark 14:9, emphasis added). Can you see any similarities between the woman's offering and Jesus' self-offering? Between her gift to Jesus and Jesus' gift to his disciples—and all of us?

3. Have you ever felt, in an especially powerful way, the magnitude of Jesus' gift to you in the Eucharist? Perhaps his words, spoken by a priest during Mass, touched your heart more deeply? Perhaps, as you received the sacred Host or drank from the chalice, you were struck by the fact that you were receiving Jesus himself? Or perhaps as you witnessed a child (maybe one of your children) receive First Holy Communion, you felt especially close to Jesus?

Enough!

Mark 14:32-52

"The hour has come." (Mark 14:41)

Now begins the real drama of the Passion. Up to this point, Mark has portrayed Jesus as being in complete control of the events going on around him. Jesus has spoken with great authority; he has healed multitudes; he has held his own against the Pharisees, scribes, and chief priests who opposed him. But now, everything changes. Jesus is no longer the chief actor in the drama of salvation. From this point on, he will become the victim, weak and passive.

Repent and Believe

To understand this shift, we have to go back to the beginning of Mark's Gospel and Jesus' first words: "The time is fulfilled, and the kingdom of God has come near; repent, and believe in the good news" (1:15). When we looked at this passage in chapter 2 of this book, we saw that the repentance Jesus preached was more expansive than seeking pardon for specific sins. Jesus was calling people to *metanoia*, a change of mind and heart. He was urging them to change the way they thought about God so they could receive the great gift of the kingdom.

But throughout this Gospel, Jesus has been running up against those who will not change their minds or hearts:

- Religious leaders who insist upon a restrictive view of God's mercy and generosity (see 2:1-12; 3:1-6).
- Crowds who are more interested in miracles and works of wonder than in embracing Jesus' teaching (see 3:7-9; 4:10-12).
- Disciples who want to limit access to Jesus and who are more concerned about their status than about being servants (see 10:13-15; 9:33-37).

It seems that almost everyone is either clueless about or resistant to the kingdom that Jesus preached:

- A kingdom where the poor are fed both the good news and real, actual bread (see 6:30-43).

- A kingdom where demons are routed and outcasts are treated with honor and dignity (see 5:1-20).
- A kingdom where everyone who believes is a brother or sister to Jesus (see 3:31-35).

This kingdom is so different from what everyone expected that the only way they could receive it was through repentance. They had to become like a "little child": open to the free gift of God's love *and* generous in welcoming everyone else who had received that love (10:15).

So here's an important question that arises from all of this: if Jesus devoted so much time to preaching this kind of repentance, wouldn't it stand to reason that he felt that real repentance was actually possible? That Jesus fully expected people to repent and believe? It doesn't make sense for Jesus to spend his life calling people to do something he knew they couldn't do. That would reduce his work of preaching and performing miracles to mere showmanship.

Enough!

This dynamic tension between Jesus' preaching and the people's response helps us understand why Mark's account of Gethsemane is so powerful.

"Remove this cup from me" (14:36). This is Jesus' final, almost desperate, plea. Ever since he began his journey to Jerusalem, he has been predicting his death. But at the same time, he has been holding out hope that it wouldn't be necessary. Even now, with his betrayer on the way and his closest disciples wrapped in a deep slumber, he is praying for a different outcome than the one staring him in the face. He wants to spare not only himself from the horror of the cross, but also everyone else from the consequences of their hardened hearts. To this end, he has never stopped trying to bring his disciples or the crowds who followed him or the leaders who opposed him to repentance.

But it doesn't come. There is no repentance. And so Jesus, seeing that all hope is gone, shifts his prayer: "Not what I want, but what you want" (14:36). *Father, you know I want to avoid all of this. But if this is what it takes to bring about true repentance, if I must allow them to deny me, betray me, reject me, and kill me in order for them to finally see how deeply you love them, then so be it. I will submit to them— and to the cross.*

Jesus returns to Peter, James, and John to find them sleeping. Again. It must have been heart-wrenching. He has just made the most important and the most fateful decision of his life, and he is confronted with the indifference of his closest friends. The ones who should have been the best equipped to support him in prayer, the ones who should have been most willing to "be slave of all" and face "the time of trial" have proved to be completely unreliable (10:44; 14:38).

Jesus has approached the moment of truth. "Enough!" he announces. "The hour has come; the Son of Man is betrayed into the hands of sinners" (14:41).

A Failed Mission

From this point on, there is no turning back. Everything happens quickly now and with a sense of tragic inevitability:

- Judas arrives with a mob sent by none other than the chief priests and scribes. These religious leaders have shown their true nature: one of violence and deception.
- One of his followers, rather than imitating Jesus' way of mercy, imitates the chief priests instead. He chooses violence instead of forgiveness, cutting off the ear of the high priest's servant. This disciple is no different than Jesus' enemies, a sign of how little effect Jesus' teaching has had on him.
- The rest of the disciples run away, leaving Jesus to face the mob alone. Just as they did during the storm at sea, just as they did when facing thousands of hungry people, and just as they did when they argued over which of them was the greatest, here too they show no sign of repentance and belief in the gospel.

It's too late. Jesus appears to have failed utterly in his mission. All that work, all that patience, all that teaching, all those miracles—and what does he have to show for it? Nothing. No one has repented. No one has believed. All that is left is for him to see his mission through to the end: to give his life as a ransom for the very people who have rejected him.

For Reflection

1. Can you point to a time in your life when you felt God was leading you to change the way you thought about him? Or maybe when you felt God was helping you change your attitude toward another person? Was it easy or hard to make that change? What role, if any, do you think God's grace played in helping you change?

2. What do you think was going through Jesus' mind the first time he found Peter, James, and John asleep? What, if anything, had changed when he came back the second time? And the final time?

3. Imagine that you are with Jesus and his disciples in Gethsemane. Unlike his disciples, you have not fallen asleep. You are concerned for Jesus because you can tell that he is upset. You want to help him, so you decide to go sit next to him and offer him some words of comfort. What would you say to him? What do you imagine him saying back to you?

Contrasting Trials and Tribulations

Mark 14:53-72

He broke down and wept. (Mark 14:72)

This has to be one of the most emotionally charged passages in the Gospel of Mark. It's wrenching to see Jesus interrogated and then brutally beaten by the chief priests and scribes. It's hard to see religious leaders act with such cruelty, and it's even harder to see Jesus become the victim of their violence. Then immediately afterward, we see Jesus' closest disciple, Peter, face his own interrogation and collapse under the weight of his own failure.

Nothing good happens here. The ramifications of Jesus' apparent failure as Israel's Messiah, which we looked at yesterday, continue on a visceral level today. The rejection by Israel's religious leaders is revealed to be more than a philosophical or theological dispute. And Jesus' own disciples' lack of faith is revealed as cowardice as well as spiritual blindness.

A Tale of Two Trials

By interlacing the stories of Jesus' trial and Peter's denial, Mark heightens the tension in both stories. He also places in sharp relief the contrast between Peter and Jesus, between the disciple and the Master. Let's set both scenes.

Jesus is standing before a hastily convened session of the Sanhedrin. The fact that it takes place in the dead of night, during the feast of the Passover, and in the high priest's private residence tells us that these proceedings are likely illegal. The chief priests know they are operating outside the Law of Moses, but this doesn't stop them. Jesus is now in their possession, and they want to move as quickly as possible. To drag out his trial would be to risk the wrath of his many admirers—the riot they feared earlier that week. Better to obtain a swift conviction and hasty execution.

While the trial is unfolding inside the house, a different trial is taking place in the courtyard. Peter, having followed Jesus from a distance, has joined the Temple guards and the servants of the high priest around a fire. Everyone is waiting for what comes next. Most likely the guards are telling the servants about Jesus' arrest, sharing in gossip about this meddlesome rabbi from Galilee and his followers. That's when one of the servant girls notices Peter and begins to question him. And this is when the contrasts become clear:

- Peter is in the courtyard facing true "accusations" about his relationship to Jesus, while his Master is in the house facing false accusations.
- Everyone in the courtyard knows that Peter is lying about being a disciple, while everyone in the house knows that they are the ones lying about Jesus.
- Peter insists over and over that he is not a disciple, while Jesus remains silent and offers no defense against the false charges thrown at him.
- Peter swears to God that he is not a disciple, while Jesus openly professes—for the first time—that he truly is "the Messiah, the Son of the Blessed One" (Mark 14:61).

Hearing Jesus' assertion, some of the chief priests and the scribes begin beating and mocking Jesus. They spit on him, blindfold him, and taunt him. All pretense of holiness and objectivity is gone as this solemn gathering transforms into an ugly, brutish lynch mob.

Meanwhile, as Jesus is being abused physically by his interrogators, Peter escapes his trial unscathed—at least physically. The cock crows a second time, just as Jesus had predicted, and Peter, realizing what he has done, breaks down and weeps. He is tortured with guilt for his failure to stand by his Master in his hour of need.

Saving and Losing

I want to take us back for a moment to the inflection point of Mark's Gospel that we discussed earlier in this book. Recall chapter 8 of the Gospel. Peter has confessed that Jesus is the Messiah, and instead of congratulating him, Jesus orders him and the other disciples not to breathe a word of this to anyone (see Mark 8:29-30). Immediately afterward, Jesus makes the first of three predictions of his death and resurrection—only to be rebuked by Peter. This draws an even sharper rebuke from Jesus, who then goes on to say,

> "If any want to become my followers, let them deny themselves and take up their cross and follow me. For those who want to save their life will lose it, and those who lose their life for my sake, and for the sake of the gospel, will save it." (8:34-35)

Now let's return to the high priest's house. This is the moment when Jesus' words find their fulfillment. Peter has sought to save his life, but Jesus has shown himself willing to lose his life for the sake of the gospel. And as we will see, Jesus saves not only his life but also Peter's life and the lives of everyone who will come to believe in him.

From the moment the Spirit "drove him out into the wilderness," Jesus has been putting himself into the position of the one who will "give his life [as] a ransom for many" (1:12; 10:45). He has poured himself out for his disciples, for the crowds, for the sick, the possessed, and the distraught. He has even poured himself out for his enemies by allowing them to hound him, accuse him, and—here at the end—to beat him and mock him. And he will continue to pour himself out right up to his very last breath.

For Reflection

1. Have you ever found yourself faced with great temptation, but you knew you should stand firm in your faith? How did you do? Did you fall as Peter did? Or did you hold fast, as Jesus did? What happened as a result of your success or failure? If you tried to "save your life," did you end up "losing" part of it (see 8:34-35)? On the other hand, if you ended up losing part of your life, what did you "save" along the way?

2. By presenting a sharp contrast between Jesus and Peter, Mark is asking us, his readers, to evaluate our own discipleship. How closely are we following Jesus? How strong will we be when persecutions and challenges come our way? Given the way Mark has portrayed Peter and the Twelve throughout his Gospel, what kind of answers do you think he was expecting?

3. Imagine that Peter didn't deny Jesus but stood up for him instead. What difference do you think it would have made to the Passion story? What difference do you think it would have made to Peter himself and to his ability to lead the Church after Pentecost?

Handed over to Pilate

Mark 15:1-15

He handed him over. (Mark 15:15)

Jesus gets shunted around quite a bit during his Passion, doesn't he?

- In Gethsemane, Judas hands him over to the chief priests and the scribes.
- At his trial before the Sanhedrin, the chief priests and scribes beat Jesus and then hand him over to the guards, who also join in the beating.
- In the courtyard below, Peter fails to stand with Jesus, effectively handing him over to his fate.

- Then, Jesus is bound once more and handed over to Pilate.
- Having found no credible evidence against Jesus, Pilate tries to hand him back to the Jews. But they refuse to accept him.
- Giving in to the crowd's demands, Pilate then hands Jesus over to the soldiers to be flogged and then crucified.

Throughout this entire ordeal, Jesus remains remarkably silent. He doesn't speak in his defense, and he does nothing to prevent his abuse and torture. Everyone who comes in contact with him rejects him and tries to leave it to someone else to decide what to do with him.

Who Is Handing over Whom?

All this would be extremely depressing if we took these events out of the context of all that Jesus has already said and done. Three times leading up to his Passion, he told his disciples exactly what would happen to him—see Mark 8:31; 9:31; 10:33-34. When answering James and John's request to sit at his right and left hand, he told them that he had come "to give his life [as] a ransom for many" (10:45). And when speaking to the chief priests and scribes—the very ones who would beat him and hand him over to Pilate—he told a parable about a "beloved son" who would be seized and killed by characters who clearly resembled the chief priests and scribes (12:6).

We might conclude that at this point, Jesus felt the die had been cast. We might think that he felt trapped by circumstances beyond his control, and so resigned himself to his fate and went without a fight.

But I don't think that's what happened. I think that, despite all the "handing over" of Jesus that everyone was doing, they were the ones who were truly trapped. They were the ones who had placed themselves on a path from which they couldn't deviate. And ironically enough, only Jesus' act of handing himself over to them could set them free.

A Deliberate Surrender

As we saw a couple of days ago, Jesus acted out on Holy Thursday everything he was going to do on Good Friday:

> While they were eating, he took a loaf of bread, and after blessing it he broke it, gave it to them, and said, "Take; this is my body." Then he took a cup, and after giving thanks he gave it to them, and all of them drank from it. He said to them, "This is my blood of the covenant, which is poured out for many." (Mark 14:22-24)

Before anyone had the chance to hand him over to anyone else, Jesus made it clear that he was the one doing the handing over. And the person he was handing over was himself. By offering his body and blood to the disciples, he placed himself—both literally and figuratively—in their hands. And by confessing that his blood was to be "poured out for *many*," he widened the scope of his gift to include people beyond those gathered in the upper room.

Very deliberately, Jesus handed himself over to the envy of the chief priests and the scribes, to the cowardice of Peter and the other disciples, to the selfishness of Judas and Pilate, to the bloodlust of the guards, and to the wrath of the crowd. He submitted himself to Gentiles and Jews alike, the ruling elite as well as everyday people, unbelievers as well as believers. And that's exactly what we're seeing in today's passage.

Breaking the Cycle

By willingly becoming the victim of people's envy and selfishness and bloodlust and everything else, Jesus took all our sins to himself and returned nothing but love and forgiveness. He came to a humanity caught in endless cycles of sin and vengeance, of giving eye for eye and tooth for tooth, and broke that cycle by refusing to retaliate.

None of this would make any difference, however, if it weren't for the miracle of Easter Sunday. If Jesus had subjected himself to all the abuse and violence thrown at him on Good Friday but then remained dead, nothing would have changed. He would have been just one of the countless victims of human sin and selfishness, another body sacrificed to placate the crowd for a few moments until they found another victim.

But Jesus didn't stay dead. As Peter proclaimed at Pentecost, it was impossible for death to hold him (see Acts 2:24). God didn't hold his disciples' sins against them. As we'll see when we read Mark's account of the resurrection, Jesus entrusted to these very deserters and deniers the good news that he "bore our sins in his body on the cross" (1 Peter 2:24).

Imagine how personal this statement was—especially coming from Peter! It was because of his sin, and the sins of the other disciples who deserted the Lord, that Jesus had to bear all the wounds inflicted upon him. It was because of Peter and the disciples' lack of faith that Jesus was left alone with no one to defend him or at least stand by him. And yet Jesus came back to them and told them, "Peace be with you" (John 20:19).

But we're getting ahead of ourselves. For now, let's just fix our eyes on Jesus, bruised, beaten, and silent, as he is handed over to the soldiers to be crucified. For Peter. For the disciples. For us.

For Reflection

1. Once more we encounter a crowd. Only instead of pressing in to touch Jesus and begging to be healed, they are distancing themselves from him and crying out, "Crucify him!" (Mark 15:13). It doesn't take much to turn them into a lynch mob, does it? Think also about the Sanhedrin as they stage their kangaroo court against Jesus. It doesn't take much for them to turn to violence either, does it? Earlier in this thirty-day retreat, I asked you to keep an eye on the crowd (see chapter 7). What

is it about large groups like this that makes them such powder kegs? Can you recall other instances when a few people were able to whip up a huge crowd into a violent mob?

2. Imagine Jesus standing there with Pilate as the crowd called for his crucifixion. What do you think was going through his mind as he took in the scene? Take a few moments to write down a prayer that Jesus might have been saying to his heavenly Father.

3. At the Last Supper, Jesus handed himself over to his disciples knowing that one was about to betray him, another would deny him, and the rest would desert him. Every Sunday at Mass, we commemorate and relive that meal. We place ourselves alongside the disciples and hear Jesus tell them, and us, "Take this, all of you, and eat of it, for this is my Body. . . . Take this, all of you, and drink from it, for this is the chalice of my Blood." The next time you're at Mass and you hear these words, imagine yourself in the upper room. Jesus sees your desire to be holy. He also sees your weakness and failings. And still he offers himself to you. After you receive Communion, find the words to express the gratitude in your heart.

Hail!

Mark 15:16-32

The inscription of the charge against him read,
"The King of the Jews." (Mark 15:26)

It may seem like a small thing to us, but to a Jew in first-century Palestine, the reference to Jesus as King of the Jews meant a lot. Nowhere in the Gospels will you find the chief priests or the scribes referring to Jesus this way, not even in mockery. In fact, the only time you see them talking about Jesus as king is at the crucifixion.

What Kind of King?

The Roman inscription that was fixed to the top of Jesus' cross read "The King of the Jews"—the very title that Pilate and the Roman centurions used to describe the charge against him (15:26). But when Israel's leaders hurled their taunts at Jesus, they called out, "Let the Messiah, the *King of Israel*, come down from the cross" (15:32, emphasis added). They saw the inscription. They heard Pilate's words. Yet they used a different title. Only a Gentile would call someone King of the Jews. Anyone steeped in the traditions of Hebrew Scriptures would have, almost automatically, inserted a more appropriate title.

That's because King of the Jews was a political title, not a spiritual one. It was a this-world title that an earthly king would take to himself. So when Pilate asks Jesus, "Are you the King of the Jews?" he's asking if Jesus is a pretender to the throne, a wannabe usurper of Roman rule. But that's not even close to describing Jesus' mission. Pilate is asking the wrong question, and so Jesus replies, "You say so" (15:2).

Jesus never wanted to be king of the Jews. He never wanted to be an earthly ruler standing alongside other political leaders such as Pilate or Herod. Instead of ruling as an earthly king—levying taxes, raising an army, involving himself in infrastructure and economic policies—Jesus' goal was to rule over the new "Israel of God," a community comprised of Gentile and Jew alike (Galatians 6:16). He came to empower those who believed in him to live in humility, love, and service—to make them into a light to the world (see John 13:34-35). And that was a very different kind of rule.

"Israel" vs. "The Jews"

During his earthly ministry, Jesus had no political ambitions. He put politics aside and spent his energy urging his fellow Jews to embrace their call to be a "light to the nations," a beacon to the Gentiles around them (Isaiah 49:6).

Jesus didn't rely on the coercive force of government to bring about the kingdom he described in his preaching. He knew that a desire to live out a covenant with God comes from inside people's hearts, not from outside, enforced through legislation. He was looking for the attractive, contagious witness of men and women whose lives reflect love of God and uncompromising love of neighbor, the heart of the covenant (see Mark 12:28-34).

This was Jesus' goal all along: a community of believers whose trust in God would help them endure the fiercest of storms (see 4:35-41). He wanted people willing to lay down their lives in humility rather than assert their dominance over one another (see 10:35-45). Jesus knew that if he could gather just a few followers willing to take up their crosses and imitate him in this form of self-giving love, their example could change the world (see 8:34-38).

What Kind of Kingdom?

Jesus began his public ministry by proclaiming that the kingdom of God was at hand (see Mark 1:15). He proclaimed a kingdom based on justice, mercy, and humility, not power, influence, and wealth. More than any other figure in Scripture, Jesus fulfilled the role of the Servant of the Lord described in the Book of the Prophet Isaiah:

> Here is my servant, whom I uphold,
>> my chosen, in whom my soul delights;
> I have put my spirit upon him;
>> he will bring forth justice to the nations.
> He will not cry or lift up his voice,
>> or make it heard in the street;
> a bruised reed he will not break,
>> and a dimly burning wick he will not quench;
>> he will faithfully bring forth justice.
> He will not grow faint or be crushed
>> until he has established justice in the earth;
> and the coastlands wait for his teaching. (42:1-4)

We can debate the practicalities of such an approach—especially given the power of sin and temptation in the human heart. But whether it was practical or not, this seemed to have been Jesus' "project" from the start: to call together a small group of disciples; teach them to live this unique, magnetic, covenant life; and use them to reach out to more and more people. The fact that he seems to have failed at this task among the people of his day—at least at this point in the Gospel narrative—is beside the point.

Enthroned on the Cross

So Pilate turns Jesus over to his soldiers for crucifixion, but not before they have a bit of sadistic fun with him. The thorny crown, the purple robe, the mock homage—it's all focused on the charge against him, that he supposedly claimed to be "King of the Jews" (Mark 15:18). This is the only charge that Pilate really cares about, and the chief priests seem more than willing to go along with the pretense in order to have Jesus executed.

But once Jesus is nailed to the cross, the truth behind their pretense comes out:

> "He saved others; he cannot save himself. Let the Messiah, the *King of Israel*, come down from the cross now, so that we may see and believe." (15:31-32, emphasis added)

They may have used the charge of King of the Jews to convince Pilate to get rid of Jesus, but they were clear: they wanted to eliminate him because of his claim to be the Messiah and the King of Israel. From the moment he burst on the scene and claimed the authority to forgive sins, Jesus was engaged in a just-under-the-surface power struggle with the religious leaders of Israel (2:9-12). Whose vision of Israel would win out? Well, here at Calvary we have our answer.

Here on the cross, even at the very end of his life, Jesus could have saved himself. But he was not the King of the

Jews, one who exercised the military or political power to destroy his tormentors. Jesus was the King of Israel. He came to win over people's hearts, not force their obedience.

Crucifixion might have been the end of the story for a would-be worldly king. But for Jesus, it was just the beginning. His act of self-sacrifice was about to usher in a new kind of kingdom—a kingdom he would rule with a pierced hand, not an iron fist.

For Reflection

1. Choose any story in any chapter in the Gospel of Mark and read it a few times. Read it closely, carefully, and prayerfully. See if you can find in this story a description of Jesus' "project" as we outlined it above. Specifically, look for ways that Jesus acted as the Servant of the Lord from Isaiah. Or look for signs of the kingdom of God that he preached—a kingdom based not on political power but on the power of self-giving love.

2. There is a powerful undercurrent in American politics that comes close to equating spiritual principles with government rule. Can you point to elements in our political discourse that lean in this direction? What do you think are some of the weaknesses of this approach? Do you see any strengths in it?

3. What does Jesus' example of kingship say to you about the way you exercise authority—in your home, at work, or even in your interior life? Are there ways that you can better live out the kind of "rule" that Jesus exercised in his ministry and on the cross?

A Torn Curtain

Mark 15:33-47

"Truly this man was God's Son!" (Mark 15:39)

Iwant to take you back to Jesus' confrontation with the chief priests and scribes in the Temple. In the wake of his casting out of the money changers and merchants, the religious leaders asked him, "By what authority are you doing these things?" (11:28). Jesus answered, first, by asking about the source of John the Baptist's authority and, then, by telling them the parable of the wicked servants. He concluded by quoting Psalm 118: "The stone that the builders rejected / has become the cornerstone; / this was the Lord's doing, / and it is amazing in our eyes" (12:10-11; see Psalm 118:22-23).

A Parable Fulfilled

Now, fast-forward to Good Friday and the scene at Golgotha. Here is Jesus, utterly and completely rejected by "builders" of every stripe: the chief priests and scribes, the political leaders of the Roman Empire, his disciples. He even appears to be rejected by God himself. But it's at this point, when Jesus is so fully rejected, that he is accepted by the least likely of characters: a Roman centurion. Mark tells us that when he saw the way Jesus died, this soldier came to the one realization that eluded everyone else: "Truly this man was God's Son!" (15:39).

Of course we have known this from the very first verse of Mark's Gospel: "The beginning of the good news of Jesus Christ, *the Son of God*" (1:1, emphasis added). God himself announced it twice—at Jesus' baptism and at his transfiguration (see 1:11; 9:7). Even the demons said as much (see 1:34). But this is the first time a human has confessed Jesus as the Son of God.

Think about this centurion for a minute. This man is another outsider. Not only is he a Gentile, but he is also an agent of the Roman government. He is a Roman *soldier,* no less, and that means he likely has blood on his hands. Finally, in his role as a centurion, he is the man who oversaw Jesus' execution. Perhaps he was the one who drove the nails into his hands and feet. It's hard to get any further outside than this fellow!

We have been tracing this theme of the outsider from very early on, and here is where it reaches its climax. From the man with leprosy to the Gerasene demoniac straight through to blind Bartimaeus and the generous widow in the Temple, Mark has shown us that the true heroes of faith are the people on the margins. The ones you would least expect to be "religious" prove themselves to be remarkably perceptive and remarkably open to Jesus' message and to his healing power.

And now comes a centurion. What's even more striking is that he confesses Jesus, not after seeing him perform a miracle and not even as he is seeking a miracle for himself. Rather, he makes his proclamation after having seen Jesus die alone and rejected.

And so Jesus' final parable is fulfilled. He, the stone rejected by all, the one who has been placed outside, is proclaimed the cornerstone by someone who himself is an outsider. And that proclamation is tied directly to Jesus' death: it isn't until the centurion sees "that in this way he breathed his last" that he understands who Jesus is (15:39).

An Empty Temple

Something else happens at the moment of Jesus' death that is also important for Mark: the veil in the Temple is torn in two, "from top to bottom" (15:38). The veil Mark is referring to is the thick curtain that separated the Holy of Holies from the outer courts of the Temple. Only the high priest was allowed to pass through that veil, and he could do it only once a year, on the Day of Atonement. And he could enter the Holy of Holies only after having performed a series of ritual cleansings and sacrifices that would make him worthy to enter the presence of the Lord.

Many scholars interpret the torn veil as a sign that the division between God and humanity caused by original sin has now been overcome. That is clearly one way to look at this, but I believe that the torn veil tells us something else as well.

Because it separated the people from the Holy of Holies, where the rite of atonement took place, the veil was the focal point for the aura of mystery that surrounded the Temple. It was the veil, this need to separate the all-holy God from a sinful people, that gave rise to the priestly apparatus and the whole system of sacrifices and offerings that kept the Temple going. But with the veil torn, that sense of mystery is gone. Gone too is the impression that God dwelt in an inner sanctum shrouded in foreboding and awe. The Temple has lost its power to enthrall. Now it is just another building, and the Holy of Holies is just another room.

The combination of the torn veil and the centurion's confession shows that God is no longer in the Temple; he is on the cross. He is present in the person of a bloodied, defeated man crying out in anguish. He is acclaimed by a man of war who keeps vigil, the light of revelation slowly dawning on him. Others are a little farther off: a small group of women—outsiders as well—who did not flee at the first sign of trouble, as Peter and the other men did.

Jesus, the stone rejected by the builders, has become the cornerstone of a new Temple, a new community of believers. Others will join them, but only after Jesus is raised up. Until then, there is just this small congregation, witnesses to an act of self-giving love that shocked, scandalized, frightened, and threatened everyone on the inside.

For Reflection

1. Just before he died, Jesus cried out, "My God, my God, why have you forsaken me?" (Mark 15:34). This prayer comes from the beginning of Psalm 22. This is one of a number of psalms of lament that portray the prayers of an innocent person being harassed and hounded. Read the whole psalm a couple of times, and try to put yourself in Jesus' place as he prays it from the cross. Are there any verses that stand out to you? What is the tone of the psalm? Bitter? Despairing? Frightened? Hopeful?

2. Read Mark 15:33-39 a couple of times, slowly and prayerfully. Jesus seems to feel that God has abandoned him, but can you find hints of God's presence and care in these verses? Look for ways that God might have been using other people or the natural world to reach out to his Son in the midst of his suffering.

3. Commentators often point to the centurion's confession as the climax of Mark's Gospel. Do you agree with their assessment? Can you point to stories and passages in Mark that back up your answer? What message do you think Mark is trying to get across by telling the story the way he does?

An Empty Tomb

Mark 16:1-20

"You will see him." (Mark 16:7)

Most scholars believe that the Gospel of Mark ended, originally, with the women running, frightened, from the empty tomb. The rest of the stories in chapter 16 are so different in style and in content from what has come before—and they are so reminiscent of stories found in Matthew, Luke, and John[4]—that the majority of commentators believe these stories were tacked on at the end in order to give this Gospel a more conclusive, happier ending.

I can sympathize with this impulse to tie things up neatly, even if it's not what Mark initially intended. I agree with the Church's decision: these closing stories are canonical and inspired by the Spirit. But I also think that we risk losing an important part of Mark's message if we don't pay attention to his original conclusion.

Occupying a Middle Ground

Mark's story of Easter Sunday begins with three women heading to Jesus' tomb around daybreak. These are the same women who had witnessed Jesus' death, but "from a distance" (15:40). There they occupied a sort of middle ground between Peter and the other men who had run away, and the centurion who proclaimed Jesus as Son of God.

We see a similar middle ground here at the tomb. That the women are showing up at all, when the men are still in hiding, shows courage and faith. But they are carrying spices to anoint Jesus' body and wondering who will roll away the stone. Clearly, they expect the tomb to be sealed and Jesus to still be dead, despite his predictions that he would rise.

When they arrive and find Jesus' body missing and a young man sitting there instead, the women are "alarmed" (16:5). They don't put two and two together and accept that he just might have risen after all. It's only what's right in front of their eyes—and what they can't see—that concerns them. Even after hearing the young man's message, they still don't believe. Rather than rejoice in the good news, they flee from the tomb, gripped by a combination of "terror" and "amazement" (16:8) They also disobey Jesus' words through the young man by saying nothing to anyone, not even Peter and the other disciples.

This reaction has been part of Mark's message all along: discipleship doesn't come easily. It's costly. It's demanding. It requires deep faith and unbending trust in Jesus' promises, even when they appear to go against all logic and everything we can see. It takes true faith to believe that "those who lose their life" for Jesus' sake "will save it" (8:35). It takes a stubborn kind of faith to believe that God would choose to save his people not by an overwhelming display of power but by surrendering himself to an agonizing death. On all three points, Jesus' disciples have failed the test of their faith. Some, like Judas and Peter, have failed spectacularly.

A New Vision

But it's here, in the midst of such failure, that Mark's message catches us by surprise. For these women, who had come to put the final seal on Jesus' death, receive a message that stuns them:

> "You are looking for Jesus of Nazareth, who was crucified. He has been raised; he is not here. . . . But go, tell his disciples and Peter that he is going ahead of you to Galilee; there you will see him, just as he told you." (Mark 16:6, 7)

You will see him. Despite their failure and lack of faith. Despite Peter's denial, Judas' betrayal, and the others' desertion. Despite their obtuseness during their travels with him. Despite everything, Jesus has not given up on them. He has forgiven them, and he wants to see them again. And more important, he wants them to see him again.

You will see him. Time and again, Jesus had called out his disciples for their blindness. But now he promises that they will finally be able to see. They will come to the kind of faith that makes revelation—Spirit-inspired insight—possible. They will come to see Jesus just as the man with leprosy, the hemorrhaging woman, Jairus, and so many other outsiders did.

You will see him. Peter once confessed Jesus as the Messiah, showing a partial vision similar to the vision of the blind man whom Jesus healed in stages (see 8:22-30). Peter knew that Jesus was a man sent by God, but he couldn't see him as a Messiah who reigned from a cross. He was expecting Jesus to overcome the power held by Pilate and the Sanhedrin with a similar, but greater, kind of power. But the cross put an end to that assumption.

Peter couldn't understand how Jesus would overcome by surrendering to death, but now Jesus promises Peter and the others that they *will* see the true nature of divine power. They will see him as the *Son of God,* as his Father had proclaimed at Jesus' baptism and his transfiguration and as the centurion proclaimed at his crucifixion (see 1:11; 9:7; 15:39).

They will see him as a Son who allows himself to be driven into the desert just as the scapegoat was driven away on the Day of Atonement (see 1:12; Leviticus 16:20-22).

They will see him as a Son who remains faithful, even unto death—even when he has been betrayed and abandoned—and who becomes the new cornerstone of the kingdom of God (see Mark 12:10). They will also see him as the *Son of Man* who "has authority on earth to forgive sins" (2:10).

They will see that he wields his authority as one who came "not to be served but to serve, and to give his life [as] a ransom for many" (10:45). They will see that the glory of this Son of Man is not the glory displayed in a burst of blinding light or in an explosion of violent power, but the glory revealed in his humble quiet acceptance of the cross (see 14:62).

Finally, the disciples' eyes will be opened, and they will come to see Jesus in a new light. And that vision will pierce their hearts and empower them to go out and proclaim his name.

In Galilee

Doesn't it strike you as odd that Jesus chose Galilee and not Jerusalem to reveal himself to his disciples? Why have them go back home? Why not honor the City of David as the place where he would first reveal himself as the risen Lord?[4]

I think Mark is doing something important by telling the story in this way. Galilee was the place where Jesus first called the disciples. It's the place where they had freely left everything to follow him. Now he is calling them back to that place where their faith was kindled so that it could be rekindled. He is bringing them back to the place of their first calling so they can hear him calling them all over again—

in a voice filled with the unique combination of absolute authority and deep tenderness and mercy that only Jesus has.

What's more, Galilee is the place where Jesus performed most of his miracles and ministered the most extensively to people. That makes it also the place where the disciples first performed miracles and ministered alongside Jesus. Jesus is bringing them back now so they can start anew—not to start all over again, but to begin from a better and different place. They have experienced their weakness and Jesus' forgiveness. Now, with the hindsight that only suffering and failure—and mercy and love—can provide, they will be able to imitate Jesus' way of self-giving love.

One more thing. I don't think Jesus means only that the disciples will see him physically when they return to Galilee. Of course they will see him and touch him again. But if Galilee is the place of miracles and ministry, if it's the place from which Jesus will send his disciples out to proclaim his gospel, then Jesus is also telling them that they will see him as they go out and fulfill their commission. They will see him in the people they will minister to: the sheep without a shepherd who are hungry, lonely, forgotten, passed over. They will see him in the sick they will pray with, in the guilt ridden who will experience the mercy of God through them, and in the prisoners trapped in their own sins or victimized by structures of injustice whom they will set free.

And You?

But all that is in the future. For now, we are left with three women running away from an empty tomb, too scared to breathe a word of what they have seen. That's how Mark ends his Gospel. Not with the exclamation mark of a joy-filled reunion or a triumphal ascension, but with a question mark: will *you* go to Galilee to see Jesus?

For Reflection

1. Around Mark's time, and for a few centuries afterward, the Church wrestled with the question of what to do with believers who fell into serious sin. Should they be allowed to receive Communion anymore? Should they be cast out of the community? Some began to wonder if these people had truly been converted and redeemed in the first place. How could someone who had repented and believed in Christ possibly fall back into sin? (You can see this dilemma spelled out in Hebrews 6:4-8.) What contribution do you think Mark's telling of the disciples' sins and Jesus' response made to the conversation?

2. The common conception of Easter Sunday is one of excitement and joy, often to the accompaniment of Handel's "Hallelujah" chorus. But Mark narrates a different story, punctuated by the women's "terror and amaze-

ment" (16:8). Are those really the only two emotions Mark wanted to convey? Where can you find the joy in his story? Where is the excitement?

3. Take a look at the other resurrection stories that were added to the end of Mark's Gospel (see 16:9-11, 12-13, 14-18, 19-20). Some are reflections of the other three Gospels, while others seem to be based on stories in the Acts of the Apostles. You can find them in Matthew 28:16-20; Luke 24:13-35, 50-53; John 20:11-18; and Acts 28:1-10. Can you find any themes or ideas in these stories that are similar to the themes or stories found in Mark's Gospel?

4. One common theme in all the Easter stories is the bedrock belief that death is not the final word. Jesus, risen and glorified, reveals that life goes on after we have breathed our last. This teaching goes against so many of our natural human instincts and fears. It also cuts through many of our assumptions and expectations for life. As a consequence, this doctrine requires a lot of faith on our part. How different do you think your life would be if the truth of the resurrection were as obvious as the truth that two plus two equals four?

Conclusion

At the beginning of this retreat, we saw that Mark pioneered a whole new way of writing called a "gospel." We considered that Mark's main concern was to preserve the stories about Jesus that the apostles had been sharing by word of mouth. But I think there is another reason Mark decided to write, and that reason can be summed up in one word. Or to be more precise, it can be summed up in one name: Paul.

St. Paul was a prolific writer. The New Testament has preserved thirteen of his letters—presuming, of course, that he wrote all the ones that bear his name. Some of his letters, such as Romans and Ephesians, are filled with complex theological arguments. Others, such as 1 and 2 Corinthians and Galatians, contain some of Paul's most passionate defenses of his ministry and the gospel he preached. And others were personal letters to other leaders in the Church, like Timothy, Titus, and Philemon.

From soaring rhetoric to finely woven prayers to harsh rebukes, Paul wrote it all. And his letters were so effective that people began to circulate them far and wide. Even St. Peter spoke of Paul's popularity and influence:

> Our beloved brother Paul wrote to you according to the wisdom given him, speaking of this as he does in all his letters. There are some things in them hard to understand, which the ignorant and unstable twist to their own destruction, as they do the other scriptures. (2 Peter 3:15-16)

Letters and Stories

"Hard to understand"—what an understatement! From the earliest days, Paul's teachings about justification, the role of the Law of Moses, and the place of Gentiles in the Church sparked controversy and, in some cases, division (see 1 Corinthians 1:10-13 for a vivid example). Of course, none of this is Paul's fault. Jesus' death and resurrection really did change everything, and change is not always easy. It's no wonder that Paul's writings aroused strong reactions, both for and against him. It's a testament to his abilities—and to his openness to the Holy Spirit—that his teachings eventually won out and became the basis for so many of the Church's doctrines and practices.

But for all the grace and revelation that Paul imparted to the Church, his contribution was limited. It was expository and polemical, and on the surface, much of it was related to concerns and practices that are no longer relevant to our lives (see, for example, 1 Corinthians 8:1-13). The deposit of faith that we cherish would be far from complete if Paul's writings were all we had.

This is the genius behind Mark's pioneering approach to spreading the good news of Christianity. Letters like Paul's explain deep, fundamental truths, but stories like the ones Mark conveyed bring these truths to life. Letters tend to follow linear logic, but stories often involve unexpected twists and turns. Letters like Romans tell us that we are justified by the grace of Christ, but stories like the man with leprosy show us flesh-and-blood people whose lives are dramatically changed by the one who is the source of that grace.

I like to think that Mark wrote his Gospel because he saw that the Church needs more than letters. It needs stories. If we're going to follow Jesus and learn to live in his love, we need more than an account of what he accomplished for us. We also need an account of Jesus himself: his miracles, his teachings, and his relationships with people like us.

That, I think, is one of the main reasons why Mark placed such a strong emphasis on Jesus' relationship with his disciples and others. As we saw earlier, Mark often referred to Jesus as teaching and preaching, but he rarely recounted exactly what that teaching was. Mark doesn't give us the Sermon on the Mount, for instance, but his stories about the widow's mite and the Syrophoenician woman teach us about the blessings that come to the poor in spirit.

He doesn't recount Jesus' "Light of the World" discourse, but he does show the difference between light and darkness in stories like Herod's feast and the disciples' blindness. Those stories stick in our memories where the Spirit uses them to stir our consciences, fire our hopes, and feed our imaginations.

Mind you, I don't think Mark disapproved of Paul's letters—or the letters of Peter, James, Jude, or John, for that matter. But I do believe that this difference between exposition and narrative is what motivated him to try his hand at something new. And as we have seen over the past thirty days, he was very effective.

A Life-Changing Story

So where does this leave us? I hope this leaves us with a deeper appreciation for Mark and his talent as a storyteller. But beyond that, I hope we are left with a deeper appreciation for Jesus and the utterly unexpected, radical nature of his message. For just as Paul had set out to do a few decades before him, Mark wanted to change the world—and he wanted to do it by changing human hearts with the story of Jesus:

- In a world that valued strength, wealth, and power, Mark wanted to show that Jesus' way of valuing the outcasts and outsiders was the true way to happiness.
- In a world filled with noisy crowds, Mark wanted to show that Jesus cherished the opportunity to minister to people one-on-one or in small groups. Rather than stir up the excitement of a crowd, Jesus sought to move people's hearts to repentance, faith, and surrender to

him: Jairus; Bartimaeus; the Syrophoenician woman; Peter, James, and John; and the rich young man.

- In a world that kept its gods locked up in temples and embodied in lifeless statues, Mark wanted to show that the one true God can never be contained or constrained. Rather than in a building or in stone, God is to be found in a living person—Jesus—and most powerfully in that living person's surrender to the humiliation and pain of the cross.

- In a world that valued those who were served far more than those who served, Mark set out to show that Jesus, God's own Son, did not want to be served. In fact, he relished serving the people he came into contact with. And he capped off his life of service, not by retiring to some long-overdue place of comfort, but by giving his life as a ransom for many.

This is the story that Mark set out to tell—"the good news of Jesus Christ, the Son of God" (1:1). May that good news, which has changed billions of lives over two thousand years, continue to change lives until the day when Jesus returns to establish his eternal kingdom.

ACKNOWLEDGMENTS

So many people have made this book possible. I can't name them all here, so I'll just thank those who had a direct influence on this project.

First is Joe Difato, founding publisher of *The Word Among Us* magazine. During the fifteen years we spent together shaping and shepherding the magazine, Joe set a high standard that continues to drive me today. His emphasis on the work of the Holy Spirit and on the need for a personal relationship with Jesus have influenced me so much that this book would not have been possible without him. I will always value his leadership and his friendship.

Then there's René Girard, the Catholic scholar who pioneered mimetic theory. I never met this man, but his insights into sacred violence and the scapegoat mechanism have had a profound influence on my understanding of Scripture. Girard's work—and the work of Girardians like Fr. James Alison and Fr. Raymund Schwager, SJ—is evident on nearly every page of this book.

There are a number of other people who were also essential to this project:

- Fr. Joe Mindling, dear friend and theological advisor to *The Word Among Us*. His patience, good humor, and theological guidance have taught me how to read a biblical text carefully and pastorally.
- Fr. Francis Martin, biblical scholar and mentor. His love for Scripture was contagious, and his rigorous classes taught me how to think critically about the word of God.
- Beth McNamara, publisher of The Word Among Us Press. Her gentle nudges and well-placed words of encouragement have proved to be invaluable.
- Cindy Cavnar, peerless editor. Her keen eye and sharp pen have made me a better—and humbler—writer.
- My children: Michael, Emma, Daniel, Tommy, Rosie, and Mark Damien Zanchettin. Their generosity assuaged any guilt I felt for not spending more time with them while I was writing this book.
- Of course, St. Mark, pioneer and Evangelist. His openness to the Holy Spirit resulted in a story that will teach, inspire, haunt, and challenge believers until Jesus returns.
- And finally, Katie, my wife: her love and her ability to bring out the good in me never cease to amaze.

I am deeply grateful for all the good things these men and women have contributed to this book.

Leo Zanchettin
July 31, 2021
The Feast of St. Ignatius of Loyola

NOTES

1. Now, this could sound scandalous to us. How could the Virgin Mary ever think that Jesus is out of his mind? But remember that Mark is a strategic storyteller. He is creating an atmosphere here. Remember also that in the twenty years between Mark's Gospel and Matthew's and Luke's, the early Church came to a much deeper understanding of Mary's role—possibly prompted by her assumption into heaven. The main point here is that whatever Jesus' family was thinking, Mark speaks of a group of people close to Jesus who didn't understand what he was about.

2. Second Vatican Council, *Dei Verbum* [On Divine Revelation], 2, emphasis added, https://www.vatican.va/archive/hist_council/ii_vatican_council/documents/vat-ii_const_19651118_dei-verbum_en.html.

3. For a brief, engaging explanation of Girard's work, see *The Theory of René Girard: A Very Simple Introduction*, by Carly Osborn (The Australian Girard Seminar, 2017). For Girard's own explanation, see his book *The*

Scapegoat (Baltimore, MD: The Johns Hopkins University Press, 1986), 95–212.

4. Luke and John portray the risen Jesus as appearing to the disciples in Jerusalem, not Galilee (Luke 24:33-36; John 20:19). I don't have time to go into the theological reasons for the differences between Luke/John and Mark/Matthew. Instead, let's do as we have done throughout this retreat and put aside the historical issues raised by these differences and stay focused on Mark and his message.